WOMEN'S HIGHER EDUCATION AND SOCIAL POSITION BEFORE AND AFTER WORLD WAR II IN JAPAN

YORIKO IIDA

Kwansei Gakuin University Press

WOMEN'S HIGHER EDUCATION
AND SOCIAL POSITION
BEFORE AND AFTER WORLD WAR II
IN JAPAN

Copyright @ 2013 by Yoriko Iida

All right reserved.

No part of this book may be reproduced in any form or by any means without permission in writing from the author.

Kwansei Gakuin University Press
1-1-155 Uegahara, Nishinomiya Hyogo, 662-0891, Japan
ISBN: 978-4-86283-126-2

Contents

Introduction 1

Chapter I: Women's Higher Education and Social Position before World War II in Japan

    1) Women's Education and Social Position before Women's Higher Education (Post Secondary Education) Begins in Japan 11

    2) Institutions for Women's Higher Education 31

    3) Tohoku Teikoku Daigaku Accepts Female Students 58

    4) Rinji Kyôiku Kaigi (a Special Committee for Education) and Some Movements Associated with Women's Higher Education from around 1917 to during World War II 71

    5) Occupations 84

Chapter II: Women's Higher Education and Social Position after World War II in Japan

    1) Education Reform after World War II and the American Occupation 93

    2) New Laws and New Education Systems 106

    3) Post War Number of Schools, Female Students, and the Courses They Selected 117

    4) Post War Situation of Female Students and Their Institutions of Higher Education 132

    5) Occupations 153

Conclusion 171

References 192

INTRODUCTION

After World War II a new Japanese constitution was promulgated in 1946 by the Japanese government after it had abolished militarism. The new Japanese constitution made clear that everyone in the nation was equal under the law and that no one was to be discriminated against because of one's religion, gender, social status and politics (Murata, 1980). There was to be democracy in Japan, support for women's rights and equality in every aspect between men and women. During the following year, new Japanese educational policies were established under the influence of the American occupation (1945–1952), and women's higher education in Japan changed a great deal. Equal opportunities in education were mentioned in the new policies and schools for higher education began coeducational policies, accepting female students. Though before World War II women were basically not allowed to receive college-level education, many new private institutions for women's higher education were established after World War II. Under the law equality between men and women was achieved and a lot of women took part in the higher education programs offered, education being one important influence affecting one's social status. In spite of this revolution in educational opportunities, there are still gaps in the social conditions between men and women, and many women have compromised their higher individual potentials to stay at lower social positions even though they had finished their higher education with much distinction by the beginning of the 21st century in Japan.

The number of women with higher education has increased dramatically since the 1960s. Since then, the percentage of women with higher education has increased more rapidly than that of men, so that in these days one out of two women goes on to institutions of higher educaton for further study. Though a lot of enterprises began to accept female workers because of high economic growth in Japan after World War II, women who had graduated with four years of college training still found it difficult to win job positions in these enterprises at their more advanced level of training. Even when they were accepted by these enterprises, their positions were generally those of assistants, helping the men to further themselves and their salaries were lower than those of the men. Because of the biased point of view that women were not suitable for positions which needed physical strength, high ability, or involved difficult decision-making, they were not offered general positions which led to future executive positions. These were only for men. Even though in 1986 the Ordinance of Equal Opportunities in Occupations between men and women was made law by the Japanese government, there are still some problems relating to the promotion of women into higher level positions. What's more, if they quit their jobs for whatever reason, it becomes very difficult for them to obtain full-time positions afterwards. Usually they can't get the same quality of job that they had and so have to accept lower paid positions.

According to the Cabinet Office in Japan (2009, February), the UN Development Program released a Gender Empowerment Measure report that explained how much women took part in society in economic and political affairs in 2008. Japan was 58 out of a list of 108 countries. This implied that women in Japan were not given enough opportunities to participate in economic and political affairs and decision-making.

Furthermore, the Gender Equality Bureau Cabinet Office (2011, January) described in *Kyôdô Sankaku* what the World Economic Forum presented in the 2010 Global Gender Gap Report. It elucidated how much women's social positions have improved. Japan was 94 in a list of 134 countries because there were still big gaps between men and women with respect to income, promotions and participation in society.

The importance of discussing this topic is that it will contribute to developing histories about women and to improving women's social positions not only in Japan but also all over the world. It will also contribute to the study of comparative education about women in the world.

According to *Josei Rôdô Hakusho* (1999), the Treaty for Abolishing Female Segregation was adopted in the 34th United Nations General Assembly in 1979. Now 163 countries take part in the treaty. This agreement discussed the equality of the sexes and the equal responsibility between men and women on household matters and childcare. The United Nations said that in order to achieve equality of the sexes, both sexes need to have equal rights, opportunities and responsibilities for developing themselves and society. The ideas of the treaty are based on the necessity of changing the traditional understanding that women have to take responsibility for household matters and childcare simply because they reproduce children. This treaty aims for social change by abolishing the idea that while men are out at work women should stay home and take responsibility for domestic work because their abilities are not sufficient to work outside of the home. It also talks about the necessity of abolishing and amending the law and habits related to female segregation and of planning some policies so that the equality of the sexes can come to be true not just formally but substantially by each nation.

After reviewing the report on the equality of the sexes in Japan, the UN Commission on Human Rights recommended that it should develop systems and laws addressing women's low income and domestic violence. It also advised that more full-time rather than part-time work should be encouraged for women because the irregular employment system has prevented the improvement of the wage inequality between men and women. What's more, it pointed out that Japan needed to create more advanced measures to prevent sexual harassment (*The Yomiuri Shimbun*, 2008).

The United Nations' programs for abolishing female segregation and improving their social status gave new energy to the development of histories about women in the world, and histories about women came to be studied from various aspects. Because studies of this topic written in English are very few, this work will help to develop histories about women and encourage people to be interested in histories of women's education and social position in Asia. Furthermore, examining historically the relationship between women's higher education and social position in Japan will suggest some of the problems those women with higher education who are contributing to Japanese society have had up to the present time and how perhaps they might improve their situations in the future. It is possible to contribute to improving women's social situations in other countries too. Finally, there are many differences in women's education between Western and Eastern countries. When we compare this item between countries, this work will give significant knowledge to researchers who are interested in women's education in Japan and Asia.

There are some publications that speak about women's higher education in Japan. These include the article "Women and Higher Education in the Japanese Empire (1895–1945)" (Harrington, 1987) in *the Journal of Asian History* and the books are *Joshi Kôtô Kyôiku no Zahyô* (Amano, 1986), *Waga Kuni Joshi Kôtô Kyôiku Seiritsu Katei no Kenkyû* (Murata, 1980), and so forth. However, the research finds very few works discussing the relationship between women's higher education and social positions in Japan. This study includes issues associated with not only women's higher education but their social positions. This work especially looks at fundamentals on Japanese culture from primary sources because there are big differences between Japan and other countries in terms of culture and people's ways of seeing things. Sometimes something is very common for the Japanese people but not for other countries' peoples at all. The study emphasizes the different points the writer recognized more clearly by comparing Japanese culture with the American (Western) one. The author would like readers to understand not only what happened in the relationship between women's higher education and social position in Japan but also the Japanese culture and way of thinking in order to continue better relationships in the future between other countries and Japan. The researcher hopes this study will be read by anyone who is not a specialist of Japanese history as well as experts in the field since as many people as possible should understand this aspect of Japan in contributing to international cultural exchange.

Regarding methodology, this work relies mainly on a number of primary documents. These are related to women's higher education in Japan and the social position of women finishing higher education, with particular emphasis on their job situation. Needless to say, primary sources have many advantages for writing histories. They enable the researcher to get as close as possible to what is actually happening during a historical event or time and the content will reflect the original document for the purposes of historical accuracy. What's more, primary sources that were compiled at the time the specific events occurred will be deemed to possess a higher status than any item written at a later date (McDowell, 2002). History is a fascinating field of study. Much of this fascination rests on the fact that historical interpretation is based on the reading of primary sources (Rose, 1977).

Because history relates to every human activity, this research used many types of primary sources, including letters, diaries, memoirs, newspapers, journals, oral history interviews, government statistics and reports, etc. History has come to be concerned with virtually every human activity (Burke, 1991).

By using statistics and reports the researcher examined how women's educational and occupational situations in Japan changed from before and after World War II. For example, we can recognize how the number of women with a higher education changed and how the number of women with a higher education who obtained outside jobs changed by seeing the comparison of the numbers from 1930 to 1960. The writer also explored the reasons for the changes in the numbers. For instance, if the numbers increased (decreased), why did they increase (decrease), or what happened at that time? From these sources, the researcher also pursued how women's interests changed. For example, what kind of subjects women were interested in learning in their higher educational institutions and what kind of occupations they wanted to engage in after finishing their higher education. Did women's interests change before and after World War II?

The author tried to understand unguarded private thoughts and emotions from diaries and memoirs by reading inbetween the lines. For example, what kind of thoughts or feelings did women pursuing higher education have before World War II? Did they have problems with other people's negative opinions against them because in those days only a few women studied in institutions of higher education, some people still thinking that women did not need to have higher (academic) education? What kind of psychological elements helped them complete their studies? In addition, before World War II women in Japan were officially allowed neither to obtain a college degree nor to study with men. There were, however, some exceptional women who had the opportunity to learn with male students and to get their degrees. Did these women experience psychological pressure from academic education and male students?

The theoretical framework of the study is to explain the relationship between a research question and its answer by examining various historical aspects related to women's higher education and social position before and after World War II in Japan. The research question is, "How did women's higher education and social position in Japan change before and after World War II? If it is still low, why has it not changed very much in spite of the large numbers of women finishing higher education?" Education is one important influence which affects women's social status. Nowadays the number of women with higher education is more than that of men in Japan. However, there are still gaps in the social conditions between the two as this research described in the very first part of the introduction. In order to improve women's social position in Japan we now need to examine the problems arising out of women's education in history. One of the ways to examine them is to investigate women's higher education in Japan before and after World War II because there is a deep relationship between social status and education. It is important to first make clear the problem of women's higher education before World War II since it is fundamental to the concept of women's higher education after World War II and from that perspective to historically look into the reason why women's social positions still remain low. In other words, this study is going to inquire about the cause of a social problem in Japan now as well as the research question in history. When we can determine the cause of a problem, it is easier to solve it. We can usually find the cause of a social problem in history. The answer to the research question is, briefly speaking, "The ideas of Japanese good wives and wise mothers (*ryôsaikenbo*), which were created by the Meiji Government (1868–1912) as the basic philosophy for Japanese women's education, are still in people's minds although the word *ryôsaikenbo* is already a dead item." The ideas soon became a national ideology in those days, continuing to be related to women's education in Japan for a long time, and even now quietly influences it without people's consciousness. In conclusion, this work presents the relationship between the ideas of *ryôsaikenbo* and the various historical aspects associated with women's higher education and social position that are stated within the body of the study.

Chapter I shows us women's higher education and social position before World War II in Japan. The common condition of women in Japan at that time was that they couldn't have the same educational opportunities as men because of their persistent secondary position in society. The first section of this chapter deals with the evolution of women's education and social positions from the Edo Period (1603–1867) through the Meiji Period (1868–1912) in Japan by explaining the educational policies of the Edo Shogunate and the Meiji Government. Although Japan officially had neither coeducational institutions for boys and girls nor women's higher education in the Edo Period, this paper focuses on private education at that time for women in the upper and upper-middle classes such as education for warriors' daughters and those of wealthy peasants. This kind of education as well as the Western education accepted by the Meiji Government came to influence women's education very much in the Meiji

Era when the Government tried to train women with Japanese characterizations which were different from those of Western women. The later ideas of *ryôsaikenbo* made up by the Government were based on these earlier education plans. In Section 2 this study presents 10 higher institutions for women established in the Meiji Period when women's higher education policies began to develop each school's main characterizations, philosophy of education, and the like. Two of these schools were set up by the Japanese government and two of them were related to Christian missions, the other six being Japanese private schools. Sections 3 and 4 point out many movements which began fighting for recognition in Japan regarding the status of women's college education between the Taishô Period (1912–1926) and during World War II (1941–1945). These movements ranged all the way from preserving Japanese traditions to liberal expressions following Western practices as introduced by individuals, missionary schools and other 'outside' groups. In the last section of this chapter the relationship between women's higher education and occupations before World War II is described. This section mainly discusses what kinds of jobs were popular among women, how many women after graduating from their higher institutions obtained jobs, and their salaries as compared with those of men in those days.

Chapter II examines the relationship between women's higher education and social position after World War II in Japan. The first and the second sections in this chapter mention how Japanese education after World War II was reformed based on democracy by discussing the American occupation and new education systems based on new laws, focusing on women's higher education. Because of this reform the Japanese education system changed from being various educational systems based on social status to that of a single-track 6–3–3–4 system. This major change contributed very much to distributing equal educational opportunities not only to ordinary people as a whole but to women as well. In fact, women's higher education possibilities improved almost immediately. Sections 3 and 4 talk about how the situation of female students and their surroundings changed after this reform by including female student attitudes towards higher education. Now, having higher education for women is not just a privilege for a small number of women but a right every woman is permitted to aspire to. In the last section the research inspects the situation of women's occupations after the Ordinance of Equal Opportunities in Occupation between men and women was established by the Japanese government in 1986. Whether this Ordinance contributes to helping women's social positions is also discussed here.

The higher education types discussed in this study deal with post secondary education levels such as *senmongakkô* (special schools), college level education before World War II in Japan and junior colleges, four-year colleges and graduate school levels after World War II. The social position of women in Japan discussion will deal with women's social conditions as compared to those of men by including some different educational opportunities and job conditions between the two sexes before and after World War II.

CHAPTER I

Women's Higher Education and Social Position before World War II in Japan

1) Women's Education and Social Position before Women's Higher Education (Post Secondary Education) Begins in Japan

In Japan, Tokugawa Ieyasu, a shogun of the Edo Era, moved to Edo (Tokyo) and established the Edo Shogunate which extended feudalism from 1603 to 1867 when the Meiji Era began. Because at that time China was more developed than Japan in almost every aspect of culture, Japan was interested in absorbing Chinese culture, ideas and so forth in order to develop its own national image. Tokugawa respected Confucianism, and incorporated his famous ideas after taking over the Japanese nation, understanding that the most important thing to govern was not military power but knowledge in such areas as morals and ethics (Abe, 1965). Confucianism advocated the importance of keeping *goringojô* (five unchanging ethics) (Sekiguchi, 1980) that were *jin* (sincerity or sympathy), *gi* (reason), *rei* (courtesy and modesty), *chi* (the ethical knowledge which decided what was good and what was bad) and *shin* (filial piety and loyalty) in order to get and keep a good relationship in society. Each of these efforts needed to be paid attention to; between a sovereign and follower, parent and child, and between couples, siblings and friends. Thus, New Confucianism mentioned that a basic concept that needed to be understood in this world was the significance of reason in all things human from the time of birth. However, since the human being also had personal feelings of desire that disrupted reason, one had to control one's desire in order to keep one's reason by learning and following moral and ethical behavior (Sekiguchi, 1980). This New Confucianism was based on the theory of *goringojô* as developed in Japan. The New Confucianism also preached the idea of *shûkochijin*, whereby a sovereign (and indeed all upper-class people) needed to cultivate the mind by learning morals and ethics so that he and they could lead their people (i.e., lower-class people) perfectly by example.

Tokugawa Ieyasu had adopted the Chinese Confucianism idea which emphasized the concept of a natural social order consisting of a clear hierarchy of classes (Fairbank, 1973) and he established the four social classes such as the warrior, the peasant, the artisan and the merchant (Ienaga, 1977). In the warrior class there were several official sub classes under the shogun and in the other classes there were some based on financial situations and backgrounds by tacit consent (Sekiguchi, 1980). Tokugawa built up a hierarchal pyramid of social forms whose top were himself, many *daimyô* (feudal lords) under him and the ordinary people under the *daimyô*. Even in the family a pyramid-form existed between old people and young people, parents and children, and husband and wife. He also advocated the importance of strict piety and loyalty in terms of ethics and morals between lower-class people, (the retainer, young people and women) and upper-class people (the sovereign, old people and men) in order to make the Edo Shogunate both stable and peaceful (Abe, 1974).

The New Confucianism became more popular than the old practices and it finally evolved into a Japanese Confucianism based on the Chinese one in the Edo Shogunate. Japanese Confucianism was more strict and artificial, exerting great pressures upon individuals. It focused on self-discipline and will power and developed an extremely strong sense of honor, duty and obligation, and dogged determination to live up to all that society expected of them. These qualities gradually spread from the warrior to other classes and the Edo Shogunate fostered not only extraordinary formalism and rigidity but also strong inner discipline and personal drive (Fairbank, 1973).

During the Edo Period the family was the basic unit of society in Japan and the most important thing to continue to preserve. For this reason, the members of the family had to sacrifice anything that would tend to end the family and its descendants (Shiga, 1977). There were many examples where members of the family gave up what they wanted to do, including marrying the person they loved, because of family considerations. The people's way of thinking came to be that they could only exist because there was a family (a house). First the family (the house) was there and then each member in it existed in order to accomplish the overall family responsibility, and thus keep one's given position (Sekiguchi, 1980).

In the family, feudal practices and hierarchal relationships also existed strongly. The father's power in the family was absolute and everyone had to follow his intentions. The first son's position was next to the father, the second son (if they had one), then the wife and finally the daughter which was the lowest position in the family. The daughter was not permitted full status as a human being without getting to a wife's position, and she had to marry a man decided by her parents. She had to follow her parents' opinions about everything and was never allowed to be against them. The position of the daughter at that time was almost the same as that of slave, and parents in the lower social positions were even allowed to sell their daughter because of poverty (Karasawa, 1978).

The relationship between husband and wife was akin to the relationship between an upper person and a lower person. Especially in the warrior's society the wife had to obey her husband completely, and strict courtesy from the wife to the husband was emphasized rather than love (Karasawa, 1978). The wife's sovereign was her husband and she had to follow and take care of him without complaint all her life, even if the husband didn't deserve to have such care from her (Shiga, 1977). The husband was allowed to have other women outside the home while the wife was never allowed to do so. Even if the husband died, the woman was forced not to remarry in her life, which people understood as simply being women's courtesy (Karasawa, 1978). In addition, at that time the wife was seen as a thing to reproduce children and she was divorced when she couldn't have babies.

Only the husband had the right to divorce. The wife couldn't even say this word. He could divorce her based on whatever reasons he liked. At that time it was still common in Japan to have the parents of the son and his family live together in the same house. The relationship between parents and sons was stronger than the relationship between the son and his wife. The parents' opinions were absolute and the couple had to follow what the parents said. If a parent didn't like his/her son's wife, that parent was allowed to force the son to divorce his wife, regardless of the son's desires in the matter.

Women's education was completely influenced by these ideas. Women were educated not to insist on their opinions but to fit into the way of the family they married into (Karasawa, 1978). Academic education for women was frowned upon (Tanioka, 1997). It was said that academic knowledge made women arrogant and prevented them from making a good marriage (Karasawa, 1978). A book at that time mentioned that it was good for women not to read. Academic education did more harm than good for women. The most required thing for women to be was gentle and obedient (Sakurai, 1943). Academic education was not required for women's education and people believed that women were much the inferior to men.

Women's education in the Edo Era focused on learning women's morals and were based on the ideas of Japanese Confucianism such as *sanjû* (three obediences) and *shikô* (four behaviors) (Sakurai, 1943). The *sanjû* meant that the woman had to follow what her father said before marriage and had to follow what her husband said after marriage. Furthermore, she had to follow what her son said in her old age after her husband died. *Shikô* meant *futoku* (Women' morals: Women should be gentle, sincere and obedient), *fugen* (i.e., Women should not talk much. Women should speak when they needed to by using appropriate language for women), *fuyô* (Women's appearance, they should always have clean clothes) and *fukô* (Women's arts: They should be good at sewing, spinning and cooking) (Sekiguchi, 1980). Following these ideas, they learned simple reading and writing, poetry, sewing, spinning, cooking, playing a music instrument, the tea ceremony, and making flower arrangements, etc. (Sakurai, 1943). However, there were differences about what women learned based on their classes. In Japan at that time there were no public schools for women (Tanioka, 1997). They learned what they needed to at small private schools called *terakoya*, the origin of future elementary schools, or from private tutors. Usually their learning period was for three to five years beginning when they were eight or nine years old (Sakurai, 1943).

There were some famous books for women's reading and writing and most of their contents were based on Chinese Confucianism. A book translated from Chinese to Japanese said that the woman's figure emphasized the absolute differences between men and women, and the relationship between the two was that of dominator and dominated. There was no doubt that the woman had to obey her husband after marriage. Because the woman could not live without a man's help, she had better not forget to thank him. Moreover, just obeying him was apparently not enough and she had to accept this relationship positively without thought of herself in order not to spoil its purity. Moreover, when it came to the relationship between the husband's parents and the wife, her obedience to them was absolute because their position was higher than her husband. When she had to choose between his parents and her husband, she needed to choose death because both of them were superior to her (Fukaya, 1981).

This book also talked about the wife's behavior whenever she remonstrated about her husband's misconduct and in such cases where she protected her family with courage instead of her husband (Fukaya, 1981). Some pages described not passive but actively strong women's behaviors and attitudes (Yajima, 2001). However, this content was not included in Japanese textbooks for the woman and they emphasized only women's obedience and patience. Japanese textbooks for women produced during the Edo Period were based not only on Chinese Confucianism but also in consideration of Japanese situations.

What's more, other Japanese books for women in the Edo Era mentioned:

1. Lessons related to training the mind: In addition to understanding *sanjû* well and being gentle, the woman should refrain from desiring anything, even if she is poor.

She should not talk much, not associate with gossip and never complain. She should not be snobbish or willful. She should be happy if someone says something good and never envy the person. Short tempers and jealousy should be avoided. Never be friendly with boys. Especially don't do anything with boys after the age of seven. Don't go out after dark. The woman's appearance should be simple (Sekiguchi, 1980). Behavior should be quiet and table manners observed whenever she has a meal (Saitô, 1986). She should be modest and mild. She should go to bed late and get up early, not being lazy (Yajima, 2001).

2. Arts: Sewing, spinning and *waka* (Japanese verses) were emphasized. Sewing and spinning are very important training. After spinning, the woman will dye the cloth and make clothes. Because finishing all this work takes time, a woman should foster diligence, concentration and patience during her work. She should also obtain a high technique, and foster a peaceful and quiet atmosphere which enhances her mind. The most significant thing is that when she sews someone's clothes, she needs to do it with the love and sincerity which are required for good work (Senjû, 1981). When creating a *waka*, because it includes many emotionally nice words, it helps that the woman be gentle, mild, obedient, kind and flexible, all of which contributes to training her mind to be useful when communicating with her husband, parents and others (Nakano, 1994).

3. Knowledge when communicating with others: The woman should neither be upset nor speak ill of anyone, but should be nice to others and benevolent in nature. She should choose good friends because they exert much influence on her. It is sensible to choose friends who are superior to her. Put others first and keep herself next to them. Respect older people and help younger people. Don't stay at another's house for a long time. Don't receive a gift from a per-

son she doesn't know (Sekiguchi, 1980).

4. Knowledge to parents-in-law: Because marriage was not simply between individuals but between families (houses), the husband's family was her own family for the woman, and her own family (or house) where she grew up was the place where she learned what she would need for her marriage (Senjû, 1981). For this reason, she had to respect her husband's parents more than her own parents, and take care of them with sincerity from the bottom of her heart. She needed always to pay attention to them and help them keep warm in winter and cool in summer. What's more, she had to sew their clothes and prepare for their meals every day. Without her husband's parent's permission she couldn't visit her own family. She was never allowed to talk back to them or be against the parents-in-law even if she was right (Sekiguchi, 1980).

5. Knowledge as a housewife: The wife should do her best in sewing and spinning. Without eating and drinking much, she should be thrifty. She should also not spend a lot of money for clothes nor waste anything. Even though her own family might be better than her husband's family, she should not mention it and so be snobbish. Always put husband's relatives first and keep hers next. Respect older sister-in-law and older brother-in-law's wife and treat younger sister-in-law and younger brother-in-law's wife nicely. She should make an effort to keep harmony in the family with sincerity and courtesy (Sekiguchi, 1980).

6. Knowledge of how to discipline her children: When a child is very young, the wife should start teaching important things (Saitô, 1986) based on *goringojô* such as *jin, gi, rei, chi* and *shin*. A mother's teaching was highly significant because it decided whether the child would be good or bad. She needed to tell her children that men and women were basically different. As for a boy, she should have him learn math

and difficult reading and writing—what was called academic education. If he needed a private tutor, she should find one. She should teach her daughter woman's morals and ethics (Sekiguchi, 1980).

These are just some examples of the content of the woman's textbooks during the Edo Period. The purpose of these books was to give lessons for the woman. She read these books again and again every day from the time she was a child (Shimizu, 1994). Finally she believed that the woman should be what was mentioned in the books and most of the women at that time followed these lessons without questioning them seriously.

In addition to reading and writing, sewing was one of the important studies for the woman then. She learned it at *terakoya* (a small private school which offered reading, writing, sewing, playing the music instruments, etc.) or *ohariya* (a small private school which offered only sewing). After learning basic things about sewing from her mother at her house, she used to enter such a school usually when 12 or 13 years old. Women started learning by sewing dust cloths and finally reached the stage where they could make *kimono* (the Japanese traditional wear). The teachers for sewing were not usually the specialists who were certified but the monk's wife and the village chief's wife who had a lot of experience in sewing. As for the students, they didn't go to such schools every day for certain periods but went there only when they needed to (Karasawa, 1978).

Moreover, some women were sometimes sent to a village chief's or famous warrior's family to learn good behaviors such as elegant languages and proper manners for a woman, which was called *gyôgiminarai* in Japanese (Karasawa, 1978). This was what we would call the woman's final education after she finished learning how to read, write and sew, etc. in the Edo Era. The main purpose the parents sent their daughters to such a family was to obtain a good marriage (Hisaki & Mita, 1981). After finishing the *gyôgiminarai*, the girl used to have a lot of proposals from rich and famous families.

This kind of apprenticeship didn't require her to do kitchen work. Her main job was cleaning and decorating rooms, taking care of guests, helping master and his wife. It was very different from being a maid and the woman usually took her personal maid to take care of her from her own house. The woman's apprentice also learned writing, drawing, crafts and music from her seniors. She could even receive a little stipend. However, because the family had to give remuneration every season to the family where its daughter was apprenticed, her family had to spend a lot of money for her learning (Karasawa, 1978).

There is a case on record where a rich, upper-class peasant family sent its daughters to some famous warrior's families. This family had three daughters and the parents sent their daughters to several noble warriors' families after they became 12 or 13 years old. The daughters were sent to three or four different families so that they would not learn only one family's manners and customs. The average length of a *gyôgiminarai* was one year or one year and a half (Hisaki & Mita, 1981).

According to a diary from this family, they spent a great mount of money for their daughters' education. When a daughter went to a famous family for *gyôgiminarai*, they had to have her bring with her every daily necessity such as a comforter, a pillow, clothes, etc. Besides this, they needed to give seasons' gifts to the warrior's family. For example, in summer and fall they gave it fruit (peaches, pears, persimmons, chestnuts, etc.), marine products, farm products produced on their land, some snacks and so forth. From April to June and from September to October they sent new clothes to their daughter and almost every month someone (the daughter's grandmother or her father) visited the warrior's family to greet them with a present. These expenses amounted to almost 15 to 18 percent of all expenditures for the three daughters (Hisaki & Mita, 1981).

However, this experience was useful for the young woman before marriage in the Edo Period where there were neither public schools nor any compulsory education. She could receive a lot of new and meaningful knowledge from the *gyôgiminarai* and thus widen her range of vision. Mostly, the daughter working at a famous warrior's family was a kind of an elite at that time and it is not too much to say that this was equal to a higher education nowadays (Hisaki & Mita, 1981).

Based on these conditions mentioned above, Japan began the dawn of women's higher education (post secondary education) in the Meiji Era (1868–1912). The Meiji Restoration destroyed Edo feudalism which had continued for more than 260 years, there-by giving up a national isolation policy and hereditary social classes such as the warrior, the peasant, the artisan and the merchant. The Japanese Emperor got the overall power again and the Government emphasized democracy politically, attending to people's freedom and men's suffrage. It focused on capitalism economically and the development of science and its applied techniques culturally (Ienaga, 1977). In this new modern society people got freedom and an equality they had never enjoyed before. As for the women, some of them got haircuts and wore the same costumes men had at that time, all of which insisted on the sense of equality between the man and the woman (Chino, 1989). Japan also received a lot of influence from Western countries after its national isolation, and it soon understood its cultural inferiority. In order to catch up with the Western countries, Japan undertook a policy for civilizing in addition to making the military stronger and developing the industries, and the core of this policy was education for the people of Japan (Uchida, Yamamoto, Okuno, & Uchida, 1986). Under such circumstances women's higher education in Japan looked to be developing smoothly at a glance.

It was *gakusei* (the school ordinance) promulgated in 1872 that permitted girls to attend the newly established public schools. "Parents were responsible for sending children (including girls) to a primary school so that there would be no citizen without education in the nation in the future. The girls had the same right of receiving education as boys did" (Katayama, 1984).

According to the Japanese government, the reason why the Government tried to have both the boys and the girls receive the same education was that the mother exercised a lot of influence over her children's first step in education and her education level sometimes decided her children's level of obtaining knowledge (Fukaya, 1981). The main purpose of this *gakusei* was to offer the same education to all children without the discrimination associated with sex and social class differences and it was based on the education system in Western countries (Uchida, Yamamoto, Okuno, & Uchida, 1986).

America's David Murray, who was invited to Japan as an adviser to the Ministry of Education, mentioned that there were two important purposes for the woman's education. One was training the woman to have enough knowledge to foster children who were going to contribute to the nation in the future. The other was offering the woman vocational education so that she could make her own life self-sufficient if need be. What's more, because the woman was suitable for teaching children by her very nature, he persuaded the Ministry of Education to establish the women's normal school which would offer the same curriculum that the man's normal school did. He also insisted upon offering the women the same education as the man in order to make the Japanese nation more modern in style (Uchida, Yamamoto, Okuno, & Uchida, 1986). Because of these reasons, after *gakusei*, the Government tried to offer the same education to both boys and girls.

We can see the Japanese government's intention from the following facts. The Government sent five girls including Tsuda Umeko to America in order to absorb the new Western culture and education and it established public middle schools for girls in Tokyo and Kyoto (Shiga, 1977) in 1872 based on *gakusei*, although these schools were closed later (Yasukawa, 1980). Generally public elementary schools and middle schools were coeducational and in 1876 there were 183 girls against 5,437 boys in public middle schools (Uchida, Yamamoto, Okuno, & Uchida, 1986) and in 1878, 93% of all girls in the middle schools were studying in the co-educational middle schools (Yasukawa, 1980).

We should not forget that not only the Japanese government but also Christian missionaries from America who visited the Japanese nation from the end of the Edo Period contributed to establishing women's education after the Meiji Restoration (1868). Around 1870, mission schools began to be established by the Christian missionaries. However, because Christianity was not allowed to be spread in the Edo Period, people still had biases about education managed by the missionaries. For this reason, at first this type of school was small in size, including only about 10 girl students at a time and sometimes including some boys. At that time the Christian missionaries' main purpose was to spread Christianity and they borrowed Japanese houses in order to do that. Soon some children who were interested in new Western ideas gathered there and they began to listen to what they were saying. They had neither special textbooks for special curriculum nor their own school buildings (Fukaya, 1981).

Gradually the mission schools for girls became more popular and bigger, and soon girls from upper-middle and high social classes were studying there (Uchida, Yamamoto, Okuno, & Uchida, 1986). These schools offered classes to the girls all in English by using books written in English, with all the teachers being American. In a boarding mission school the students wore Western dresses and talked to American teachers, had Western meals served, and were treated like American ladies. The school strictly kept morning and evening worship every day, the Sabbath every Sunday and included Christian customs and ethics about everything they did (Fukaya, 1981).

Because the curriculum of mission schools for girls in Japan followed that of American schools, the level of content for the subjects was high, and equal to liberal arts levels in colleges in Japan now (Uchida, Yamamoto, Okuno, & Uchida, 1986). The girls also learned morals which were very different from the morals they had formally learned and believed without question from their families. For example, Christian lessons denied Japanese old thinking that the woman was inferior to the man and that she had to follow her husband all her life, even if he was very barbarian and didn't deserve to have her help in taking care of their children. The Christian lessons advocated that the man and the woman were completely equal and they needed to observe monogamy, persuading their students that a human being's happiness should be based on sincerity without cheating. These schools required students to have independence and responsibility as the human criterion. In addition, they were taught that spiritual intelligence was much more important than wealth and authority in order to achieve happiness. The Christian lessons helped the woman at that time to experience an enormous spiritual revolution and understand that men and women were the same human beings when facing problems or making big decisions (Yonekura, 1977).

In that society most people thought that girls didn't need an academic education because they still believed in the woman's morals established by the Edo Shogunate, which had continued for more than 260 years. It was also thought that education in primary schools was not helpful for the woman and boys' and girls' studying together in the same school was not a good idea. Because of the people's ways of thinking, the percentage of girls entering primary school at that time didn't increase as the Ministry of Education in Japan had expected (Katayama, 1984). According to the Ministry of Education, the percentage of girls entering primary school changed from 15.14% of all girls in 1873 to 22.10% of them in 1880, while that of the boy's changed from 39.90% of boys in 1873 to 61.21% in 1880 (Table 1) (Uchida, Yamamoto, Okuno, & Uchida, 1986).

As for middle schools for girls managed by Christian missionaries, because Christian lessons and their education were strongly connected, the girl graduating from these schools couldn't adjust to a society which still had old Japanese customs and morals and so people began to frown on these girls (Uchida, Yamamoto, Okuno, & Uchida, 1986). Though Christian missionaries very much contributed to middle school education for girls in Japan, their education was very different from traditional Japanese education and the women educated there became like American women. These schools were like foreign countries. Since they ignored teaching sewing and cooking (what we call domestic education), and emphasized learning English, the women graduating from such schools didn't know how to sew the *kimono* or cook. They asked a tailor to sew their *kimono* and the cook to cook for them. It was not always the case that every girl graduated from this type of school married a man of high social standing where all domestic work was done by those trained for such work. If she married a diplomat, learning English might be useful. But in fact, because most of the girls married peasants and merchants, learning English had little meaningful use for them. Christian lessons made such women avoid producing children, which was very bad for the Japanese nation's future (Mochizuki, 1892).

In 1881 a revised school ordinance, named *kyôikurei*, was promulgated and it said that because boys and girls were basically different, they should receive a different type of education, especially in moral discipline, so that boys would become brave men and girls would become calm women (Katayama, 1984). In order to increase the percentage of girls' entering primary school, the Ministry of Education in Japan added sewing and handicraft to girls' curriculum and decreased the time spent in arithmetic, and other classes, in consideration of the opinions of people in society (Tanioka, 1997). The Ministry of Education prescribed that the curriculum for girls in the primary school education needed to include two to six hours of sewing and handicraft lessons in a week by reducing or excluding some of the other classes. For example, in 1891 pupils had classes in moral discipline, reading, composition, writing, arithmetic, social science (including Japanese geography, Japanese history and foreign geography), science, drawing, music, physical education and sewing and handicraft (only for girls). The boys had five hours a week in arithmetic, four hours of social science and three hours of physical education while girls had four hours of arithmetic, three hours of social science and two hours of physical education during the same period. In addition, as they became upper-classmen, the number of classes in writing and science for girls decreased, compared to that for boys, and the number of the classes for sewing and handicraft increased (Kaneshige, 1979).

Table 1 : The number of children in primary schools and the percentage of children entering primary schools

Year	the number of children in primary schools			the percentage of children entering primary schools	
	boys	girls	total	boys	girls
1873	879,170	266,632	1,145,802	39.90	15.14
1874	1,297,240	417,528	1,714,768	46.17	17.22
1875	1,462,059	464,067	1,926,126	50.49	18.58
1876	1,540,841	526,960	2,067,801	54.16	21.30
1877	1,594,742	568,220	2,162,962	55.97	22.48
1878	1,671,276	601,948	2,273,224	57.59	23.51
1879	1,717,422	597,648	2,315,070	61.34	23.24
1880	1,762,113	586,746	2,348,859	61.21	22.10

Source: "Meiji ki no joshi kyôikukan no kenkyû", *Kanazawa Daigaku Kyôiku Gakubu Kyôka Kyôiku Kenkyû*, 1986.

Regarding the middle school education for girls, the Ministry of Education in Japan said that middle school education for boys and girls should definitely be different. Henceforth, middle schools should not be coeducational and the curriculum between boys and girls should be different. The girls' curriculum included moral discipline, women's courtesy, reading and writing, drawing, sewing, handicraft and music but excluded English and math. In 1891, the name of the middle school for girls was changed to *kôtô jogakkô* (girls' higher school), making a distinction from the middle school for boys (Uchida, Yamamoto, Okuno, & Uchida, 1986).

However, people still complained that the content of *kôtô jogakkô's* curriculum helped the girls obtain only knowledge that had no practical element. *Kôtô jogakkô's* education was not useful for daily life for all people. The content of *kôtô jogakkô* education applied only to girls from high society and the big cities, while the motivations behind these girls were to find good marriages or to help satisfy their vanity (Nagano, 1988).

Later, the girls' level in the content of those subjects in common with boys and girls was fixed lower than those of boys and later, the period of girls' middle school education became shorter than that of boys by one year. These policies were organized so that girls' levels in the content of the subjects wouldn't become higher than those of boys. This lack of intellectual content in the same subjects for girls grew generally larger and larger (Tanioka, 1997). The main curriculums at *kôtô jogakkô* at that time were changed into housekeeping, childcare, physiology and hygiene, which were much more emphasized than academic education (Uchida, Yamamoto, Okuno, & Uchida, 1986).

Because of being too early westernized for too short a period, people in the early Meiji Era couldn't catch up with the new educational situations being developed in Japan. For this reason, the society pursued again the old Japanese style of education for the women and criticized Western education. Education based on Japanese Confucianism came back in spite of some criticism against it and it emphasized chasteness, dearness, charity, obedience and diligence, insisting that chasteness was the most important for the woman. It decried debauchery, trouble, haughtiness and negligence. It also advocated that the woman should foster her morals, focusing on moral discipline (Uchida, Yamamoto, Okuno, & Uchida, 1986).

Some educational ideas for the woman at that time mentioned that the right education for women was supporting the woman who achieved her duties and responsibilities 'for our society' (Uchida, Yamamoto, Okuno, & Uchida, 1986). We needed a balance between a positive and a negative thing in the world as we had between day and night. Because the man's position was positive while that of the woman was negative, the man should be outside to work while the woman should be home to take care of domestic work. Since this was the natural order, it was the woman's way and duty to follow and help her husband obediently in keeping chasteness. In addition, it was a woman's significant role to take care of their children (Fukaya, 1981).

Considering people's opinions mentioned above, the Japanese government concluded that Western education for the woman didn't fit Japanese women because the Japanese economy had not caught up with those of Western countries and the situation between Western countries and Japan was not the same. In order to develop the Japanese nation Japanese girls needed to learn more of those women's morals advocated since the Edo Period to foster her spirit. Education for the woman focused on moral discipline for women and academic education was thought of lightly again. The new nation's policy for girls' education was in helping the girls be self-conscious as a Japanese girl and fostering the woman who had only Japanese womanly ideas at heart, avoiding Westernized ways of thinking (Uchida, Yamamoto, Okuno, & Uchida, 1986).

This policy led to the idea of educating the Japanese woman to become the *ryôsaikenbo* (Tanioka, 1997). The meaning of the *ryôsaikenbo* was that of the woman who could educate her child to contribute to the Japanese nation in the future and the good, sincere, simple housewife who could build up a happy family, paying close attention to keeping the house clean and harmonious (Uchida, Yamamoto, Okuno, & Uchida, 1986). This education for the woman came not from the democratic concept that she should be educated as a person in the same way the man was, but from the idea that she needed to be educated in order to support her children and help her husband by understanding the different roles between the two (Katayama, 1984).

The *ryôsaikenbo* was a historical complex created through the special process of Japanese modernization from the Meiji Restoration (1868). It was complex indeed, mixing Japanese nationalism with the woman's ideal figure based on old

Japanese ideas associated with Japanese Confucianism. The Japanese nation was a big family organized by an Emperor (master) and citizens (subjects). The relationship between the two meant harmony based on love and respect for each other. The citizen had to be faithful to the Emperor whatever might happen (Fukaya, 1981). In order to develop the nation, Japan needed to focus on developing its economy by fostering a stronger military and by improving its industries. The nation was based on individual families where the children were trained and encouraged to contribute to Japanese development in the future (Yamamoto, 1974). Because the wife married not only her husband but also the household (family) of the husband, she had to follow her husband as wife and reproduce and bring up the successor of the house and the nation as a mother should (Fukaya, 1981). The duty of the woman as a citizen for the nation's development was managing the family, fostering children by following her husband and understanding the differences between the man's role and that of the woman in society (Uchida, Yamamoto, Okuno, & Uchida, 1986). The idea of women contributing to the nation came from Western ideas and it was not part of the Japanese imagination earlier (Fukaya, 1981). The idea of *ryôsaikenbo* limited women's positions to those of wife and mother and this idea permeated the public completely around 1900, continuing to take over in the Japanese society until after the close of World War II.

2) Institutions for Women's Higher Education

The contribution of Japanese government to women's higher education in the Meiji Era (1868–1912) was to establish a women's normal school, not because the Government had tried to offer higher education to women previously but because it needed teachers who could offer secondary education to girls (Tanioka, 1997).

In 1875, Tokyo Joshi Shihan Gakkô (Tokyo women's normal school), whose purpose was to bring up elementary-school teachers, was established by the Ministry of Education in Japan. Since women were suitable for taking care of children, the Japanese government found it necessary to train qualified female teachers. This school was the highest institution for women's education and it was to play a central role in developing women's higher education at that time (Murata, 1980).

The women, specifically between 14 and 20 years old, were allowed to enter this school but sometimes women younger than 14 and older than 20 were permitted to study there as well (Makiishi, 2000). In 1875 when 74 female students entered this school, most of them were given scholarships for their tuition and subsistence from the Japanese government. Five years were required to finish school. The main curriculums of this school were geography, history, physics, moral discipline, chemistry, education, economics, natural history, mathematics, and composition, and the sub-curriculums were the arts, music, physical education, handicraft, and so forth. Regarding the main curriculums, each course had ten levels to reach and pass and the students who passed all of them were awarded official certification. During the course of training, every six months they had to pass a new and more difficult exam in each subject in order to advance to the next level (Ochanomizu Joshi Daigaku 100 nenshi Kankô Iinkai, 1984).

This normal school was a boarding school whose first floor had classrooms, a president's room, and a faculty room and whose second floor was the students' dormitory. The dormitory featured study rooms and bedrooms, each room being shared by seven students. It also had a dining room, a hairdressing room and bathrooms. The school building was in the Western style having tables and chairs, very different from a traditional Japanese style such as working on *tatami* (straw mattresses). There were many students who had their very first experience of sleeping on a bed (usually people slept on tatamis in Japan at that time) and some of them fell out of their beds with the thunder of castanets. One problem associated with the meals was eating beef. Because most of the students were not used to eating beef, they found it difficult to get used to. The school had told them that they should eat beef since it had a lot of good nutrition. However, there were some students who felt sick just hearing the word "beef" (Ochanomizu Joshi Daigaku 100 nenshi kankô Iinkai, 1984).

In 1880, twelve women's normal schools were established by the Japanese government. They were Niigata, Chiba, Yamanashi, Gifu, Hirosaki, Akita, Kanazawa, Toyama, Fukui, Matsue, Tottori and Tochigi women's normal schools. There were very few graduates at first. Less than 20 students out of a total of 1000 enrolled in all schools graduated every year because Japanese society at that time thought little of women's education and female teachers, and because the course work was very hard for the women, without due recognition of their efforts, to complete their studies in order to become teachers. For these reasons, the women's normal schools discussed above were united with the men's normal schools in each prefecture and independent women's normal schools disappeared. In 1885, Tokyo Joshi Shihan Gakkô was also united with Tokyo Shihan Gakkô (Tokyo normal school) because of financial problems and it was redesignated as the women's section (Murata, 1980).

Around 1885, because this school gained a lot of influence from a revised school ordinance (1881), the curriculums themselves were changed from purely intellectual contents to those focusing on women's moral discipline. Instead of five years to finish the assigned coursework, the time was changed to three and half years and still later to only three years. The curriculum included courtesy in addition to moral discipline, and housekeeping instead of economics, eliminating history. As for natural history, physics, chemistry and geography, the number of these classes was reduced and the level of content material lessened. In the dormitory the students were required to cook for themselves in order to learn domestic work, an important requirement by then for all women to pursue (Ochanomizu Joshi Daigaku 100 nenshi Kankô Iinkai, 1984).

In 1886 the Ministry of Education in Japan allowed this school to prepare secondary school teachers (Makiishi, 2000) and its name was changed from Tokyo Joshi Shihan Gakkô to Tokyo Joshi Kôtô Shihan Gakkô (Tokyo women's higher normal school). Four years were required to finish the course work after students completed their secondary education and at first it was not divided into sections. In 1889 the Ministry of Education decided to divide this coursework into three sections such as literature, science and technical art, including sewing so that students could pursue their professional skills. In the same year a two-year extension program was established after finishing the four-year course in order to encourage students into further study. In addition, courses were established for kindergarten teachers in 1895 and provisions for teacher training for secondary education schools were established in 1902 because there were very few institutions for training kindergarten teachers in spite of the number of existing kindergartens, and because the number of the students at secondary schools had almost doubled after 1894 (Murata, 1980).

In 1890, Tokyo Joshi Kôtô Shihan Gakkô again became independent of Tokyo Shihan Gakkô since it was argued that men and women were basically different, and there were some problems related to the dormitory's management after they had united (Murata, 1980).

Because of the social developments after 1895, right up to when Japan defeated China in the Sino-Japanese War in 1907, many girls tried to receive secondary education. In 1899 there were 37 *kôtô jogakkô* with 8,857 students enrolled, while in 1907 there were 133 *kôtô jogakkô* with 40,273 students enrolled (Ôtani, 1993). For this reason, the Government needed to establish a new women's normal school to train female teachers to teach these girls. The Japanese government focused on the national feeling that the Japanese nation was a big family organized by an Emperor (parent) and citizens (children). Because the nation was based on individual families, respecting and keeping the family was important in order to develop the nation. The woman's duty as a citizen was to manage the family, raise the children and follow her husband. The Japanese government included these ideas and the idea of *ryôsaikenbo*, which by 1900 had permeated the public mind completely, into their design for women's education.

In 1908, Nara Joshi Kôtô Shihan Gakkô (Nara women's higher normal school) was established by the Japanese government in Nara Prefecture in the west of Japan. This school emphasized not only developing students' intellectual knowledge but also offered certain disciplines to raise the standard of women's morality as well. Women with morals should be virtuous, calm, obedient, elegant, noble, simple, orderly, quiet, careful, thrifty, and affectionate (Nara Joshi Daigaku 60 nenshi Henshû Iinkai, 1970). Generally, the woman's main job in life was to give birth to and bring up her children well after marriage as a good wife and a wise mother should for developing the country. The Japanese nation established this school in order to produce female educators who were going to be good models for women who would be able to help their children become good adults (Ôtani, 1993).

The students who were allowed to enter this school were selected by governors of prefectures and by the president of this school. Selections were very competitive and only the best students from every school were chosen. At Nara Joshi Kôtô Shihan Gakkô, students had to take first a four-month introductory course before their three-year and eight-month main course (Nara Joshi Daigaku 60 nenshi Henshû Iinkai, 1970). This four-month introductory course existed until 1914. In this course students had to learn moral discipline, Japanese, Chinese, a foreign language (English), mathematics, drawing, music, sewing, and gymnastics. In addition to these subjects, they had a class offering the geography and history of Nara Prefecture, the role of Nara as capitol of Japan in the eighth century and school excursions around the area (Ôtani, 1993).

According to one student's memory about the four-month introductory course, the English classes were very tough for students. The English teacher, who was herself Japanese, seemed to think that these girls were very smart and so she gave them a large English assignment every day. The students paid close attention to their English studies and they used to have English vocabulary cards with them even with their meals, in addition to studying English hard until late at night. By summer, many students looked pale and were absent from school because of sickness. It was a big problem in the school at that time. After realizing that the cause of the sickness was a psychological breakdown from too many English assignments, the English teacher herself became panic-stricken, always asking the students about their situations and saying that she didn't want them to be sick (Ôtani, 1993).

Promotion from the introductory course to the main course also called for passing very severe exams and it was not always that every student could enter the main course of instruction. More than one student recollected feeling uneasy while waiting to see whether she had passed or not. The main coursework was divided into four sections such as Japanese and Chinese, geography and history, mathematics and science, and natural science and household matters. The Japanese and Chinese section required students to learn Japanese, Chinese, history and penmanship. After a few years most of the students in this section could read and write Chinese, some even composing Chinese poetry. The geography and history section included the subjects of geography, history, Japanese, Chinese, law and economics. The mathematics and science section contained math, physics, chemistry and handicraft. The natural science and household matters section offered the students botany and zoology, physiology and hygiene, mineralogy and geology, household, physics and chemistry. Students in every section also had to learn moral discipline, education, English, music and gymnastics. In addition, they had to choose one subject out of drawing, music, sewing, handicraft, gymnastics and gardening. This school aimed at developing teachers who had general knowledge (Nara Joshi Daigaku 60 nenshi Henshû Iinkai, 1970).

In order to instill the disciplines to become women with a woman's morals, Nara Joshi Kôtô Shihan Gakkô instituted a boarding system. (Later, only those third graders and second graders who had their houses in Nara City were allowed to commute.) In the dormitory, strict schedules were organized. For example, students had to get up between 5:30 and 6:30 A.M. and come back home by 5:00 to 6:00 P.M. The time for study and going to bed was also decided. Three meals were cooked by the students by turns every day and there were no staff people to cook and clean the dorm. Domestic affairs were a duty for every student during her stay in the dorm. These schedules were organized in order to help the students not only become calm, kind women with a woman's morals but also learn about the whole household as women's designated domestic work (Nara Joshi Daigaku 60 nenshi Henshû Iinkai, 1970).

This boarding school's system was also based on the idea of Japanese nationalism focusing on the family. There were five buildings in the dormitory area and the students were divided into 22 groups. Each group seemed to be a kind of family having a leader, with the role of father, and a sub-leader, who had a role of mother. These leaders were chosen from older students who were good at both scholarship and personality. These buildings were completely in Japanese style, having *tatami*, a lobby with arranged flowers inside the front door, a living room with pictures, bedrooms, study rooms, bathrooms, a garden with season's flowers and so forth. Learning the family system there, the students helped each other in order to develop their own concepts within the family environment (Gunjishima & Takaguchi, 1992).

Women's higher education in modern Japanese history began to be discussed in earnest in the early part of the 20th century when *senmongakkô* started to be established, which were post secondary in education level (Mizuno, 1982). In 1903, the Ministry of Education promulgated an ordinance creating *senmongakkô* which offered to its students a higher level of achievement in the practical arts. As an entrance qualification, the students had to graduate from a middle school (in the boys' cases) or a *kôtô jogakkô* having more than four years of study in the curriculum (in the girls' cases). The length of study in these special schools was at least three years and, in some, four years graduation (Tokyo Joshi Ika Daigaku, 1966).

Four schools were established in this era that still exist as famous women's colleges even now. They are Joshi Eigaku Juku established in September 1900 (today, Tsuda Juku Daigaku[1]), Tokyo Joi Gakkô set up in December 1900 (today, Tokyo Joshi Ika Daigaku[2]), Joshi Bijutsu Gakkô founded in April 1901 (Joshi Bijutsu Daigaku[3]), and Nihon Joshi Daigakkô (Nihon Joshi Daigaku[4]) (Tanioka, 2000).

On September 14 in 1900, Joshi Eigaku Juku (girls' English school) was established in Tokyo by Tsuda Umeko who was born in Tokyo in 1864, the second daughter of Mother Hatsuko and Father Sen, the latter having had an experience over time with an English interpreter at the Edo Shogunate. From the time she was eight until she was 19 years old, Tsuda Umeko studied abroad in America with four other girls, absorbing Western culture and education, all under the Japanese government's support (Oba, 1990). In 1882 when she was 18 years old after finishing elementary and secondary education in America, Ms. Tsuda came back to Japan (Suzuki, 1994). She quickly noticed in Japanese situations that there was a big gap between men and women and that the men had absolute power over the women. The women there didn't have independent minds and there were almost no schools for the women (Shibukawa, 1970). From the time she began to teach English at Kizoku Jogakkô (girls' school for

---

[1] Tsuda College
[2] Tokyo Women's Medical University
[3] Joshibi University of Art and Design
[4] Japan Women's University

aristocracy), she was not satisfied with the students who were not diligent enough to suit her in spite of their advantages from a high society. Perhaps because of this, from this time on she began to evolve her ambition to found a higher educational school for women from ordinary families. In 1889 when she was 26 years old, she left for America again and studied biology at Bryn Mawr College. Because the purpose of her second visit abroad was also to learn how to teach, she also learned the principles of education at another normal college. Three years later she came back to Japan and taught at Tokyo Joshi Kôtô Shihan Gakkô until 1898 (Tsuda Juku Daigaku Sôritsu 90 shûnen Kinen Jigyo Shuppan Iinkai, 1990).

Through these experiences, Ms. Tsuda finally set up Joshi Eigaku Juku. When the school was opened at first, there were only 10 students there. At the very beginning, before these incoming students, she mentioned that true education required a teacher's positive attitude with a solid grounding in the subject and students' positive attitudes toward wanting to study, rather than fancy facilities. Moreover, offering classes in small sizes was important to developing individual students' ability (Tsuda Juku Daigaku Sôritsu 90 shûnen Kinen Jigyô Shuppan Iinkai, 1990). She aimed at training women who should complete themselves, sharing roles equally with men and holding jobs to develop the society (Tsuda Juku Daigaku, 1960).

A graduate from this school remembered that Professor Tsuda had great talent as an educator with her independent and positive nature. In class she always taught her students with great passion, checking their English translation into Japanese again and again, and considering each word's nuance until she was satisfied with it. Her attitudes toward teaching were always powerful (Shibukawa, 1970).

The basic policies of Joshi Eigaku Juku were: 1. Offering

English education and training female English teachers whose skills needed to reach the requirement of the Ministry of Education in Japan, 2. Organizing the atmosphere like a family where the president, instructors and students lived together so that instructors helped the students evolve into ladies who were sound and had good behavior, and who were familiar with various issues.

In order to foster all-round women, this school offered not only English education but also music, drawing and lectures discussed by experts from various fields. Students were told to always be modest, polite, gentle, and calm, pursuing their studies (Tsuda Juku Daigaku, 1960). In addition, Tsuda Umeko included character education based on Christianity and recommended that the students and instructors take part in worship before class every day and on every Sunday. Bible study was also included in the English class. In the dormitory, students had opportunities to learn penmanship and sewing on Saturday afternoons (Shibukawa, 1970).

In 1904 Joshi Eigaku Juku was permitted as *senmongakkô* and the following year the Ministry of Education allowed the students from this school to become English teachers without taking the national examination for teachers. Only Joshi Eigaku Juku was allowed to have this special permission from the Japanese government and it continued until 1923 (Tsuda Juku Daigaku Sôritsu 90 shûnen Kinen Jigyô Iinkai, 1990). This meant great achievements for this school's graduates and Tsuda Umeko. Until 1929 when she died, she had offered her whole life to this school's development (Shibukawa, 1970).

On December 5, 1900, Yoshioka Yayoi, the twenty-seventh female medical doctor to be trained in Japan, established Tokyo Joi Gakkô (Tokyo women's medical school) as a women's occupational institute (Ikeda, 1966). She was born in 1871 in Shizuoka Prefecture and her father was a doctor of

Eastern medicine there (Suzuki, 1994). Because of her father's influence she wanted to become a medical doctor from a young age. When 24 years of age, she married a man who also was qualified to practice medicine and had run some schools. When they opened the female medical school, there were only four students in a small classroom (Shibukawa, 1970).

The reasons why Yoshioka established this female medical school were that only one medical school which had allowed women to study had shut out female students because male students in the school sometimes seduced and attacked them as well as the fact that the school had some other problems with discipline associated with female students. She herself had studied medicine there and was always insulted by male students, the reason being that she was a woman. She wanted to offer women who wanted to learn medicine a place where they could study freely without the pressure of men. She also considered international political relationships between China, Korea, Taiwan and Japan. After the Sino-Japanese War (1894–1895) many high-ranking officials from these countries came to Japan with their wives. Since at that time their wives were unaccustomed to having medical examinations from male doctors when sick or delivering a baby, female medical doctors had an important role to play to keep a good relationship between these countries (Shibukawa, 1970).

Yoshioka wanted to train female doctors who were at the same level professionally as the male doctors and who established financially independent positions after completing their vocational education (Tokyo Joshi Ika Daigaku, 1966). She always told her students to study hard. She gave lectures lasting for six hours and she required her students to study by themselves for six hours a day because medical study was the most difficult subject to complete satisfactorily

(Ikeda, 1966). It was not just a subject they learned but a duty they used to save people's lives. The main policy of this school was to help students recognize the importance of lives and how to deal with them as well as offering medical techniques (Murata, 1980). At first she taught physiology and anatomy while her husband offered physics and chemistry (Aoyanagi, 1992). Yoshioka demanded that her students study hard while she also was a very active teacher. She not only offer lectures to the students but also allowed them to observe her own delivery when she gave birth to her first son. She used herself as prime material for experiments for her students to learn from (Shibukawa, 1970).

After the ordinance for the *senmongakkô* was promulgated in 1903, the Ministry of Education in Japan revised the medical school ordinance. The new ordinance said that from 1914, only students graduating from a *senmongakkô* would be allowed to try the national medical examination. Formerly the examination could be taken by anyone who felt qualified to try (Shibukawa, 1970). Because Tokyo Joi Gakkô had to be closed, not having been promoted to *senmongakkô* status, it applied to the Ministry of Education for permission to function as a *senmongakkô*. However, the Ministry of Education rejected it saying that a women's medical school was not needed (Murata, 1980). Ms. Yoshioka visited the Ministry many times to negotiate this issue. Finally, since the Ministry of Education said that the *senmongakkô* should be managed not by private persons but by a juridical foundation, Yoshioka established a juridical foundation by converting all the assets of their property into this foundation. In 1912 this school was permitted to be a *senmongakkô* and in 1920 became a school specified by the Ministry of Education, which meant that the students graduating from the medical school were allowed to become medical doctors without passing the national medical examination. The Ministry of Education in

Japan at last understood this school's hard work and successful achievement (Shibukawa, 1970). This school accepted not only Japanese female students but also students from China, Korea and Taiwan, and by 1940 about three thousand female medical doctors graduated from there (Tokyo Joshi Ika Daigaku, 1966).

Joshi Bijutsu Gakkô (women's art school), which became *senmongakkô* in 1929, was established in Tokyo on April 1st in 1901 (Ikeda, 1966) by Fujita Fumizô, Yokoi Tamako, Tanaka Shin and Taniguchi Tetsutarô. It was Ms. Yokoi Tamako who was the most important person contributing to the establishment of this school. She was born in 1853 and began to earn many forms of education associated with art and so forth from the age of fifteen. She learned Western sewing, Western cooking, Japanese sewing, Japanese cooking, Western painting, water painting, playing the koto (Japanese traditional musical instrument), the tea ceremony and flower arrangements. In 1889 she started to teach students Western sewing, Western painting and cooking in a Christian *jogakkô* (Satô, 1999). She spent the next 16 years of her life as an educator and was a Christian activist seeking to improve women's social position. Before then she had wanted to establish a women's art school in order to develop women's social status and their independence through the art medium she loved so much (Joshi Bijutsu Daigaku, 1980). The ideas behind establishing this school included modern concepts such as social service based on Christian benevolence, women's independence with working and abolishing women's discrimination (Satô, 1999).

The purpose of this school was to train female art specialists and female art teachers. Art very much influenced the development of a nation and the art of a nation represented its civilization, its progress and its characteristics. Although from olden times Japan had loved art and tried to develop it, art education was only available for men, ignoring the woman. Now it was the duty of the country to improve the woman's art sense in order to develop the country as well. This school would begin to compensate for the lack of women's art education and to bring up female artists who could teach at women's normal schools and *kôtô jogakkô,* they being independent spiritually and financially (Joshi Bijutsu Daigaku, 1980).

This special school had a two-year higher course plus an added two-year research course (a post secondary education level). The higher course had a Japanese art section, a Western art section, a carving section and a design section in addition to ethics, education, Japanese, mathematics, a foreign language, art history, and art analysis as minor subjects. This curriculum enjoyed advanced content (Joshi Bijutsu Daigaku, 1980).

In November, 1901, a women's art association was established and the first women's art exhibition was held. According to *Tokyo Nichi Nichi Shimbun,* this exhibition had great success by accepting women as participants and it would become a good opportunity to develop Japanese women's art education in the future (Joshi Bujutsu Daigaku, 1980).

After Ms. Yokoi's death in 1903, this school was taken over by Ms. Satô Shizuko who was the housewife of a medical doctor. Her ideas of education focused on individual guidance in small classes and in a boarding school. She tried to get in touch with students individually by occasionally staying at the dormitory herself. She believed that students could enjoy friendship and be unified through art in the dormitory. Their lives were devoted to pursuing beauty by using their whole bodies and thus creating beauty itself. Basically her purpose was to foster women who were good wives and wise mothers with a strong sense of beauty in many different fields (Ikeda, 1966).

After World War I (1914–1919) this school built a new school building at Kikuzaka, Tokyo. Surrounding this school were an olden time samurai (warrior)'s mansion and Tokyo Teikoku Daigaku (Tokyo Imperial University) to the east. Looking southward the students could see people's houses and Mt. Fuji on a fine day. To the west there were modern Western type hotels with granite and brick and illuminations on their roofs shining after dark. Famous Japanese writers often stayed there at that time and this area was, what we called, 'artists' town.' There were coffee bars with red and blue lights at night where the students used to spend time relaxing. Some of the students sometimes went to see silent movies with human voices coming from behind the screen. In such surroundings the students freely developed their talents for artistic expression (Nagai, 2000).

In 1901 a new arrival, this one a man Naruse Jinzô, returned from study in America and recognized the necessity for an institution for women's higher education, and so established Nihon Joshi Daigakkô which became *senmongakkô* in 1904, Tokyo. When he opened this school at first, 222 students entered it. The students' backgrounds were various and the age of the students from 18 to 34 or 35 years old of age. Some of them had just graduated from *kôtô jogakkô* while others were already teachers and housewives. The students were gathered from various prefectures (Aoki, 1981).

There were three main goals in this school: 1. Emphasizing liberal arts for becoming a good person. 2. Helping students obtain qualifications for jobs by giving students intellectual, moral, and physical education to become the 'perfect' woman. 3. Developing abilities to perform those duties in the nation to become a faithful citizen (Murata, 1980). Though these policies included new Western elements, they basically focused on Japanese nationalism and the idea of *ryôsaikenbo*.

Naruse's theories for education were based on his practical ethics and sociology, which were sourced from what he learned in America. Regarding his practical ethics, he asserted that human beings grew by learning through their experiences in the outside world and by making efforts through their will and passion to support their purposes. These elements—will, passion and practices, were most important for people's growth (Kageyama, 1994). Because women had been told they were inferior to men and not smart, few thought they could do anything great, which prevented the women from becoming successful as people. However, if the woman had a positive attitude (or a kind of desire), for example, to complete a big thing, and practice it with strong will and passion, then such a person would be able to develop her talent and finally reach success. It was this voluntary drive that was the most important element for women's education (Yamamoto, 2001). Naruse applied this theory of education to women's ethics and morals rather than to academic achievement. Such a woman obtained perfect ethics and morals for herself after having engaged in voluntary practices with a strong will and passion to complete her positive goals.

When it came to his theory of sociology, Naruse mentioned that there was a strong relationship between society and individual people and we shouldn't think that they were separated. The society existed for individual people and such people existed for society. Society helped them develop and they, in turn, contributed to society's development. A sound society fostered sound people and they supported the sound society. In Naruse's case the meaning of society included the Japanese nation. His sociology was not sociology as a special science but sociology based on the ideas of Christian ethics and practical philosophy with an ethical passion for improving society (Yamamoto, 2001). For Naruse, improving society meant improving women's higher education in order to produce women with enough knowledge to individually contribute to society.

This school had three courses including home economics, literature and English, as well as a pre-class for English, and three years were required to finish. Naruse was the first person that established home economics as a main course. He deplored the fact that women's higher education in Japan was behind the times when compared with that of America and thought that promoting women's higher education was very important in citizenship making and making society in Japan a better one (Murata, 1980). In order to build up better citizens and society in general (the Japanese nation), one needed to foster women who could nurture better families contributing to our country's development. In order to make better families the woman should learn home economics at a higher education level. In this course, students learned natural history, physiology, physics, gardening, psychology, ethics, education, child study, art history, social science, sociology, law and economics. This course aimed at training the woman who could be independent financially and spiritually and have talent enough to improve the society with voluntary practices (Akatsuka, 2000).

Before these four schools were established, women's higher education in Japan was supported by Christian mission schools organized by foreign missionaries (Tanioka, 2000). Mission schools for women's higher education in Japan were always pioneers in thought about women from the 1870s to 1945. Education systems and methods born in Western countries were transferred to Japan through them and these schools were supported by a lot of money from foreign countries. These schools emphasized a high quality of liberal arts and small class size, such as 10 students to a class. The older mission schools in Japan were established mainly at Tokyo, Osaka, Yokohama, Kobe, Nagasaki and Shimonoseki.

Later, other schools were situated in Sapporo, Hakodate, Hirosaki, Sendai, Maebashi, Kanazawa, Hiroshima, Nagoya, Shizuoka, Okayama and Fukuoka. Especially so was Kobe Jogakuin (Kobe College), which was permitted as a *senmongakkô* soon after the ordinance for *senmongakkô* was promulgated in 1903, and Tokyo Joshi Daigaku (Tokyo Women's Christian University) was famous (Tanioka, 1997).

Kobe Jogakuin was established by Ms. E. Talcotte, the first president of this school and Ms. J. E. Dudley in 1875 in Kobe, Hyôgo Prefecture, west of Japan. Both of these women were from the Women's Board of Missions in America and were teachers for a while after graduating from their schools (Kobe Jogakuin 100 nenshi Henshû Iinkai, 1977). Though their main purpose was to introduce Christian practices in Japan, at first both women were surprised at the low social status of Japanese women and wanted to do something to improve it based on Christian ideas (Kobe Jogakuin 100 nenshi Henshû Iinkai, 1982).

When Ms. Talcotte and Ms. Dudley opened the school, there were 26 students, three living in a dorm and 23 commuters. Soon it became a boarding school where teachers and students lived together because they thought that sharing many things in a residential setting was helpful in having students understand Christian ideas (Kobe Jogakuin 100 nenshi Henshû Iinkai, 1977). The students were raised in a Japanese atmosphere in the dormitory so that they could always understand Japanese society easily when conveying Christianity. In the dormitory they usually used Japanese simple furniture without beds and tables (Kobe Jogakuin 80 nenshi Henshu Iinkai, 1955). Ms. Talcott and Ms. Dudley emphasized Bible study and conveyed Christianity rather than an academic education as most important (Kobe Jogakuin 100 nenshi Henshû Iinkai, 1977).

The second president, Ms. V. A. Clarkson arrived at this

school in 1877. She graduated from Mt. Holyoke Seminary and had had some teaching experience. She thought much of academic education through liberal arts and tried to raise the curriculum level upward. She thought the perfect education should be established through both faith and high intellectual knowledge. However, due to ill health she retired from this school and went back to America a few years later (Kobe Jogakuin 100 nenshi Henshû Iinkai, 1982).

Ms. E. M. Brown and Ms. S. A. Searle took over her ideas and raised the academic level in all the liberal arts and in active Christian missionary work as well (Kobe Jogakuin 100 nenshi Henshû Iinkai 1982). This school brought up a number of great teachers by using Western educational methods from Wellesley and Smith Colleges in America, which were different from the system of normal schools in Japan (Hatanaka, 1999). Ms. Searle also focused on students' religious activities and recommended that the students do service at church schools on every Saturday and have no classes on that day.

Kobe Jogakuin offered four-year post secondary education. The first year students learned Bible study, Japanese, Chinese writing, English, mathematics, gymnastics and after that they had to take required courses, courses associated with their major subjects and elective courses. The required courses were Bible study and gymnastics. The students chose their major subjects out of Japanese and Chinese writing, philosophy, biology, chemistry and mineralogy, and English (later music and housekeeping were added). Regarding the elective course, they picked out one subject from Japanese, Chinese writing, mathematics, history, translation, Germany, music, drawing, sewing. These classes were usually offered all in English (Kobe Jogakuin 100 nenshi Henshû Iinkai, 1977).

Ms. C. B. Forest, the fifth president, very much emphasized international exchange for international friendship though the spirit of loving human beings as friends had already been spread in the school since it was established. In 1924 when the Oriental Exclusion Act was passed by the Congress in America, she and the faculty of this school sent a letter to America complaining that this decision was against the Christian intentions to avoid unfriendly behavior and race discrimination. After this Act Kobe Jogakuin positively tried to keep international friendship going between America and Japan in order to lessen political tension between the two countries. For example, Rockford College in Rockford, Illinois, Radcliffe College in Cambridge, Massachusetts, and Lake Erie College in Painesville, Ohio became sister schools of this school and they exchanged letters, pictures, magazines organized by the students, and art works. In 1928 when Japanese art was introduced in the Rockford student year book "The Copula," the art club in Kobe Jogakuin helped this event. This school also accepted American scholars and researchers who were interested in Japan and Asia by offering $1000 to each person and it sent some of their Japanese students to Olivet College and Mount Holyoke College through the system of exchange students. Moreover, this school sent the students to international meetings such as The Pacific Christian Student's Conference in California in 1936, The World Federation of Educational Associations in San Francisco in 1923 and in Tokyo in 1937, annual summer conferences of Japan and American students were held alternately in Japan and America from 1934 through 1940 (Terasawa, 1991).

The idea of founding Tokyo Joshi Daigaku was decided by general conference at the 50th Anniversary of Protestant Christianity's arrival in Japan. It was held by Japanese Christian unions and mission unions from other countries in 1909 in Japan. The following year this idea was proposed and decided in a world Christian meeting held in the United Kingdom (Tanioka, 1997), and in 1918 Tokyo Joshi Daigaku was established as a women's higher educational institute by six Christian organizations from America, Canada, England and Japan. One of the purposes of founding this school was to have a Christian university in Asia that was not associated with any specific organization (Tokyo Joshi Daigaku 80 nenshi Henshû Iinkai, 1998).

Because these organizations were looking for a person who was a Japanese positive Christian, a famous person recognizing global situations, who understood women's education with aspirations to be a president of the school, Nitobe Inazô, a professor at Tokyo Teikoku Daigaku, was chosen (Tokyo Joshi Daigaku 80 nenshi Henshû Iinkai, 1998). Ms. Yasui Tetsu, a graduate of Tokyo Joshi Kôtô Shihan Gakkô, a Christian and a positive educator, who had the experience of study abroad in England, was chosen as a dean (and later, the second president). An Amercan, A. K. Reischauer became a director (Tanioka, 1997).

When this school opened, there were 76 students: 37 of whom were from Christian *kôtô jogakkô* and 45 who were Christians themselves. The purpose of this school was to offer higher education to women in Japan based on Christian precepts. However, there were no intentions to make students Christian or insist that they work in the church. This school encouraged them to obtain intellectual knowledge with a spirit of sacrifice and service that each of them would eventually bring to the country, the society, or the family (Tokyo Joshi Daigaku 80 nenshi Henshû Iinkai, 1998). Speaking there on opening day, Nitobe said that this school emphasized individual achievement based on Christianity, respecting insight rather than book knowledge, good personality rather than scholarship, and the person rather than the talent (Shibukawa, 1970).

Tokyo Joshi Daigaku had four courses such as English literature, humanities, Japanese literature and practical business. The humanities included Western elements and had subjects for cultivating human beings in order to obtain high common knowledge, offering summaries of philosophy and outlines of the arts. The practical business coursework aimed at training women for jobs to help people without a lot of extra benefits attached to the work. It had two sections, one for business and one for charities. Requirements for all courses were practical ethics, bible study, gymnastics and outside lectures during the week (Tokyo Joshi Daigaku 80 nenshi Henshû Iinkai, 1998).

In 1923 Ms. Yasui took over the position of president (Suzuki, 1994) because of Nitobe's too tight schedule. She described four educational policies: 1. Training good personalities based on Christianity. 2. Focusing on gymnastics. 3. Developing liberal arts. 4. Keeping good harmony between academic life and social life. She did not support strict dormitory rules with strict oversight because she wanted to respect each student and allow each one to consider her options freely. Usually, student dormitories in Japan were bound by strict school rules but Yasui didn't think it was a good idea. This was what she learned from her study abroad in a college at Oxford, England where students' lives were free without many rules but the students maintained public order (Shibukawa, 1970). In order to develop the liberal arts, she set up a three-year higher course in addition to post secondary education. She mentioned that this course was aimed not at offering academic education so that students could receive specific jobs but at training women who could cover any type of work with enough knowledge and a serious attitude (Tokyo Joshi Daigaku 80 nenshi Henshû Iinkai, 1998). She was a great educator who left her mark on this school until 1941 when she retired (Shibukawa, 1970).

By 1920 there were some *senmongakkô* whose main characteristic was focusing not on Western style education but on Japanese style education based on the ideas of a good wife and wise mother. Famous schools of this type were Jissen Joshi Gakuen (Jissen Women's Educational Institute) and Kyôritsu Joshi Gakuen (Kyôritsu Women's Educational Institute).

Jissen Joshi Gakuen was established in 1899 by Shimoda Utako who was born in 1854 in Gifu Prefecture (Jissen Joshi Gakuen 80 nenshi Henshû Iinkai, 1971). When she was born, she was named Seki but she received the name of Utako from the Empress herself. She worked with the Emperor's family and once, when she presented her poem before the Empress, that lady liked it so much she named her Utako whose meaning is 'reciting' in Japanese. She was from a scholar's family; her great-grand father, grand father and father all were scholars of Chinese classics. She was a very smart girl despite her young age, writing in verse when five years old and describing poetry when six or seven (Naki Shimoda Kôchô Sensei Denki Henshûsho, 1989). From the age of 19 to 26 when she married, she worked under the Emperor's family as a tutor because of her talent. After her husband's death, she was chosen as a dean for Kizoku Jogakkô. Tsuda Umeko also was teaching English there after coming back from her study abroad in America. When Shimoda was the dean there, she had been to Western countries to inspect their education systems (Shibukawa, 1970). After recognizing that women's education in Japan was undeveloped through her trip, she decided to establish a school not for girls from the aristocracy but for ordinary girls in order to develop the country (Naki Shimoda Kôchô Sensei Denki Henshûsho, 1989).

In 1889, Shimoda established Jissen Jogakkô and Joshi Kôgei Gakkô (industrial art school for girls) in Tokyo and they became Jissen Joshigakuen after their union in 1908. It was subsequently promoted to *senmongakkô* status in 1925. When this school was opened at first, there were 40 students in both schools. The main policy of Jissen Jogakkô was fostering good wives and wise mothers by offering practices required for women's morals and housekeeping. Jissen means 'the practice' in Japanese and the meaning included in the school's name was practicing or executing something based on what students learned. This meaning also related to practical ethics including realism from Western countries and practical discipline from Confucianism (Jissen Joshi Gakuen 80 nenshi Henshû Iinkai, 1971).

Joshi Kôgei Gakkô emphasized training women who made their lives by themselves by offering practices and technical arts (Jissen Joshi Gakuen 80 nenshi Henshû Iinkai, 1971). Shimoda's basic ideas were bringing up perfect Japanese-type women rather than training new women who were educated based on Western philosophy and Christianity. Women didn't have to study in order to earn material things equal to what men had (Amano, 1986). However, there were some women who needed to work and to help their families because of poverty. This school contributed to these women, but it was not good for the women to concentrate on their interests, ignoring domestic work (Shibukawa, 1970). Shimoda especially focused on developing Japanese women's moral character, such as a faithful wife based on Japanese nationalism in both schools (Jissen Joshi Gakuen 80 nenshi Henshû Iinkai, 1971).

Kyôritsu Joshi Gakuen, whose name at first was Kyôritsu Joshi Shokugyô Gakkô (Kyôritsu women's vocational school) was established by Miyagawa and other people in 1886 and became a *senmongakkô* in 1925. The meaning of Kyôritsu is "cooperation," and this school was founded by many people's cooperation (Takase, 1956). Though he was a teacher at Tokyo Joshi Kôtô Shihan Gakkô, he didn't like the way that its principles changed whenever its dean changed. Due to this reason he wanted to organize a private school which would offer education to students based on concrete principles (Shibukawa, 1970). The purpose of this school was training women who studied vocational technology while improving their behavior. The policies of this school were focusing on teaching high-level technical arts, offering some other subjects in order to develop students' common knowledge and enriching women's morals (Takase, 1956).

Kyôritsu Joshi Shokugyô Gakkô had four courses such as sewing, knitting, embroidery and artificial flower arrangements. The students had to choose one or two courses while learning professional techniques. When sending their works to a universal exhibition held in Paris in 1889, to a national exhibition in 1890 and to an exhibition in Chicago in the US in 1893, the students received prizes and so the name of this school came to be known throughout the world. Because especially the course of artificial flower arrangements received such a high reputation, the school established a special system whereby students in this course could obtain scholarships covering all their tuition and expenditures. Only those students who passed the one-month preparation course would continue (Takase, 1956).

In 1911, Kyôritsu Joshi Gakuen set up the course of training technical art teachers for secondary education. Its curriculum included moral discipline (i.e., contents based on Japanese Confucianism), education, Japanese, housekeeping, sewing, bags and pouches, knitting, braids, embroidery and artificial flowers. Since graduation from this course was very difficult, only 38 students out of 53 were allowed to matriculate at the first commencement. Later, the Japanese government specified this school for training temporary teachers after the increase in the number of secondary schools (Takase,

1956).

The next year, the course of housekeeping was set up for training the most intelligent students who had talent to manage a family after finishing their secondary education. This course was organized by Hatoyama Haruko who graduated from Tokyo Joshi Kôtô Shihan Gakkô and who later became a president of this school. But this course had no relationship to vocation. This was a kind of preparatory school for marriage and the curriculum was organized for fostering good wives and wise mothers (Takase, 1956). There were sewing, cooking, cleaning, embroidery, knitting, artificial flowers, inserted flowers, music and the tea ceremony (Shibukawa, 1970), and students were required to be self-controlled and obedient by keeping strict rules for their daily dress (Amano, 1986). In 1914, the number of students graduating from this course was only 43, in 1928 the number of graduates had risen to 1,627 (Takase, 1956). In a short time, this school became a famous *senmongakkô* that offered special learning arts and fostered future good wives and wise mothers by teaching women's morals and building up good teachers for secondary education (Shibukawa, 1970).

Though in 1920 there were only 10 *senmongakkô* for women, some 46 schools were permitted as special schools in 1935. The number of female students there increased from 1670 in 1920 to 13320 in 1935. In 1922, six public special schools were established in Fukuoka Prefecture, Osaka Prefecture, Miyagi Prefecture, Kyoto Prefecture, Hiroshima Prefecture and Nagano Prefecture. This was a big change because before then there were only two national normal schools for women's higher education. The number of private medical schools increased from one to three; two private schools for dentistry and six for the pharmacy were added. Before, women's higher institutions were mainly for training teachers (e.g., English, elementary and secondary schools, sewing) but gradually, fostering women's medical doctors, dentists and pharmacists were focused on. In 1925, 39.4% of students in the special schools belonged to home economics, including sewing and handcrafts. Also, 37.7% of them worked in the humanities (Japanese and English literature) and 22.1% of them were at medical schools. Though in 1915, the percentage of students who belonged to home economics including homemaking was only 12.7%, it reached 41.1% by 1930 (Amano, 1978).

However, these special schools were established at a lower level than colleges where only men were allowed to study at that time and they constituted a side route or inferior channel in the system of higher education. Even regular women's schools were situated as a lower level institution than those of men's higher education and they were not allowed to offer any degrees to their students (Yoshino & Kusano, 1999).

3) Tohoku Teikoku Daigaku[5] Accepts Female Students

It was Tohoku Teikoku Daigaku's science department that first accepted three female students in 1913 (Tohoku Daigaku, 1960). This university was established by the Japanese government in Sendai City, Miyagi Prefecture in 1911 after Tokyo Teikoku Daigaku in 1869 (Tokyo Daigaku 100 nenshi Iinkai, 1984) and Kyoto Teikoku Daigaku[6] in 1897 (Kyoto Daigaku 100 nenshi Henshû Iinkai, 1998) were set up. The purpose of these three universities at that time was not to offer mass education but to train a very few elite people who would work in government as public officials with high positions or as special technicians. For this reason, only a few qualified men were allowed to study at an imperial university and nobody expected that women would be accepted there. This was a very big incident which caused a great impact on Japanese society and women's higher education in those days.

Mr. Sawayanagi Masatarô was the president of Tohoku Teikoku Daigaku in 1913 and it was he who opened the university to the three female students. He had been a secretary, a chief secretary, a chief of bureau, and finally Vice-Minister of the Ministry of Education in Japan after graduating from Tokyo Teikoku Daigaku and he had had experience in teaching ethics and psychology at several *senmongakkô,* in addition to being the president of some *senmongakkô* and some normal schools for men (Seijô Gakuen Sawayanagi Masatarô Zenshû Kankôkaihen, 1980).

Sawayanagi's way of thinking toward women's higher education saw it as equal to studying special high-level voca-

---

[5] Tohoku Imperial University
[6] Kyoto Imperial University

tional techniques. For him, only those women who would need to work at a vocation in the future should have the same higher education as men did because they were required to use the same knowledge and techniques as men needed to use once they had a job. There were no gender differences there (Hirano, 1978). He also said that it was not common for a woman to have a vocation and some people even thought that the woman who had to have a job was unhappy because generally having a job meant no marriage and at times no family. The family was the origin of happiness for human beings and a happy society should be composed of happy families where a man and a woman lived together by helping each other (Yoshino & Kusano, 1999). If a woman married and became a housewife, she didn't need to have a higher education. However, if a woman had to have a job in her life, then it was very important for her to have the same higher education the men received. Sawayanagi mentioned the necessity of higher education for women who would need to have a job in the future in *Tokyo Asahi Shimbun,* November 4, 1912, saying that Tohoku Teikoku Daigaku would accept a female student who wanted to study chemistry (Tohoku Daigaku, 1960). Sometime previous, he had written in his personal notes that female students who had enough ability to obtain advanced knowledge should be accepted by an imperial university after they passed the same entrance exam offered to male applicants (Sawayanagi, unidentified).

Then why was Sawayanagi able to carry out this big incident almost independently without express permission from the Government to accept the three female students, not as subsidiaries but rather as regular students who were allowed to obtain their Bachelor's degree after completing their studies with full Japanese approval? There were some differences between prescribed items offered to applicants at Tohoku Teikoku Daigaku and those at Tokyo Teikoku Daigaku and Kyoto Teikoku Daigaku. Tokyo Teikoku Daigaku and Kyoto Teikoku Daigaku only allowed a student graduating from high school or having the same knowledge as the student graduating from high school to enter these schools, while Tohoku Teikoku Daigaku welcomed in not only this type of student but also students from *kôtô shihan gakkô* or *senmongakkô*. Tohoku Teikoku Daigaku chose students by requiring them to have the same examination as the student from high school when the university didn't have enough new students to fill their beginning classes (Murata, 1980). Regarding the *kôtô shihan gakkô* and the *senmongakkô*, Tohoku Teikoku Daigaku picked out eight schools in 1911 and 24 schools in 1913. The university said that because there were a lot of talented students from other institutions besides high schools, it would accept students from other institutions having the same quality of basic knowledge as the students from high schools. This school considered less where the students came from and more on their ability to cover the requirements of the university (Kageyama, 2000).

In those days, Japan had some education systems which were different from the usual single system such as six years for elementary school, three years for middle school, three years for high school and four years for college—what we call the 6–3–3–4 system. For example, when it came to the education system for boys, six years for elementary school was obligatory for everyone and five years for middle school, which was not obligatory. There was a two-year post-elementary course for a student who didn't opt to go to middle school. After finishing middle school, a boy had two choices. One was to go to a *senmongakkô* for three or four years and the other was to go to high school for three years in order to prepare for the imperial university. In the latter case a student was allowed to go to high school after he finished four years of education in middle school. He didn't have to finish a five-year curriculum in middle school. High school was a kind of preparatory school for university, in other words, only students who were planning to go to university had to go to high school. There had been no way for *senmongakkô* students up to then to be allowed to enter university. However, Tohoku Teikoku Daigaku permitted those students it picked out from those graduating from *senmongakkô* to enter this school. Under the education system for girls, six years for elementary school was obligatory and a two-year post elementary course, the same as for boys. A girl who wanted to have further education went *kôtô jogakkô* for four or five years after finishing their six-year elementary education and then girls' *senmongakkô* for three or four years more. Because there was no high school for girls, they had been shut out from studying at university. But possibilities of studying there were born for the girls after Tohoku Teikoku Daigaku permitted the students having teaching certification for normal school or secondary education to try their entrance examination when the university didn't have the numbers of students for entrance.

Sawayanagi focused on this positive point. No mention of girls not being allowed to study there was ever recorded in the prescribed rules of Tohoku Teikoku Daigaku. In 1913, although Sawayanagi transferred to Kyoto Teikoku Daigaku as its president, the next president of Tohoku Teikoku Daigaku, Mr. Hôjô Tokitaka, accepted the following three women as students for regular courses by taking over Sawayanagi's plan (Tohoku Daigaku, 1960). They were Ms. Tange Mume, 41 years old, Ms. Kuroda Chika, 30 years old and Ms. Makita Raku, 26 years old (*Tokyo Asahi Shimbun*, 1913). Tange was born in Kagoshima Prefecture in 1873. After graduating from a normal school, she learned home economics in Nihon Joshi Daigakkô. In 1911, she was the first woman who could pass a chemistry teaching exam for a secondary education level, which was offered by the Ministry of Education (Suzuki, 1994). When she was an assistant professor of Nihon Joshi Daigakkô, she was accepted for a chemistry course at Tohoku Teikoku Daigaku (Murata, 1980). Kuroda was born in Saga Prefecture in 1884 and entered Tokyo Joshi Kôtô Shihan Gakkô in 1906. After finishing post secondary education and a research course, an extension program after the post secondary education there, she was appointed an assistant professor of the school (Suzuki, 1994) and accepted by the University for their chemistry course. Makita, graduating from the research course of Tokyo Joshi Kôtô Shihan Gakkô, was accepted by a mathematics course. Because their *senmongakkô* and higher normal schools were not chosen by Tohoku Teikoku Daigaku, their status was as applicants who had teaching certifications for secondary education (Murata, 1980).

According to Kuroda's memory, after getting information that Tohoku Teikoku Daigaku would accept female students, Mr. Nakagawa, the president of Tokyo Joshi Kôtô Shihan Gakkô, recommended to Makita to try the examination. Tange and she were persuaded by Dr. Nagai, a professor at Tokyo Joshi Kôtô Shihan Gakkô and Nihon Joshi Daigakkô (Yukawa, 1994). Dr. Nagai visited President Nakagawa's office and asked him to recommend Kuroda. Though she was very interested in studying at Tohoku Teikoku Daigaku, she was worried about the examination because she had heard the chemistry course was very competitive. Dr. Nagai cheered her up by saying that Tange would also try this examination. First, however, they had to have an English examination and another competitive examination after passing this. The English exam had two parts; one was oral and the other was writing. The oral examination consisted of an interview and a reading component between a teacher and three students. That night she couldn't sleep well because of her concern about the result of this exam. Fortunately, after Tohoku Teikoku Daigaku was satisfied with the results of the three women's English examinations and further competitive ones, it allowed them to study there as students for regular courses (Kageyama, 2000).

It was the Ministry of Education in Japan that was very much surprised at this information. Mr. Okuda, the Minister of Education at that time, said that the Ministry of Education thought of these women as auditors who would not get Bachelor degrees in the future (Yukawa, 1994). It was true that there was no exact mention of prohibiting female students from studying there as regular course students. However, it was understood that 'a student' in the prescriptions of imperial universities meant only men. They were not sure then whether they were going to allow the female students to obtain their Bachelor degrees in the future (*Tokyo Asahi Shimbun*, 1913). Finally, the Ministry of Education said that they were going to accept them as students for regular courses but that this was a special example. It didn't mean that the Ministry of Education permitted either coeducation or female students' study in imperial universities (Yukawa, 1994). Acceptance of female students by the Ministry of Education was greatly influenced by Sawayanagi, who still had power there and by the fact that at first Tohoku Teikoku Daigaku didn't have enough numbers of male applicants at that time because Sendai, where this school was located, was in the countryside, which was not so charming for young students (Tohoku Daigaku, 1960).

Public reactions about this issue were varied. *Osaka Mainichi Shimbun*, on August 22, 1913, reported that the Ministry of Education was always conservative and negative when dealing with a new issue. Why did the Ministry of Education hesitate to give Bachelor degrees to the three women in the future? The women should be treated the same as men. We should pay tribute to Sawayanagi's contributions and the efforts of the three women. Not only Tohoku Teikoku Daigaku but also other institutions should open their gates to female students. According to *Tokyo Nichinichi Shimbun* on August 24, 1913, Ms. Hatoyama Haruko mentioned that university education made female students neither arrogant nor aggressive and there were already many women who had Bachelors degrees in Western countries. This was significant progress for Japanese education and society. *Yorozuchôhô Shimbun*, August 24, 1913, also pointed out that women were never inferior to men. If a woman had enough ability to learn at a university, universities should be opened to her, respecting her social economic position. On the other hand, someone at *Tokyo Nichinichi Shimbun*, August 22, 1913, described that university education was too much for women because their duty for the nation was just to deliver and educate their children. Situations in Japan were different from those of Western countries (Taishô Shôwa Shimbun Kenkyûkai, 1966).

In 1916, Kuroda and Makita became the first women Bachelors of Science in Japan. Tange was a little late in receiving her B. S. degree because of illness (Kageyama, 2000). After obtaining the B. S. degree, Ms. Kuroda was accepted by Tokyo Joshi Kôtô Shihan Gakkô as a professor and in 1921 she went to Oxford University in England to study for two years. In 1929 she received a Doctoral degree in science from Tohoku Teikoku Daigaku and became a professor emeritus at Ochanomizu Joshi Daigaku (Tokyo Joshi Kôtô Shihan Gakkô's new name after World War II) in 1952. She devoted herself to the study of science until 1968 when she died, a pioneer of Japanese female scientists to come (Suzuki, 1994).

Ms. Tange went to graduate school in Tohoku Teikoku Daigaku after receiving the B. S. degree because she was such a good student. After finishing graduate school, she remained there as an assistant. In 1921 the Ministry of Education sent her to Johns Hopkins University in America in order to study nutritive chemistry and she earned a Ph.D. In 1929 she was accepted by Nihon Joshi Daigakkô as a professor and received another Doctoral degree in agriculture. She also spent her whole life in study as a scholar (Suzuki, 1994).

Ms. Makita married an artist, Mr. Kaneyama, after teaching at Tokyo Joshi Kôtô Shihan Gakkô for a while and gave up all her studies in order to become Mrs. Kaneyama. On the other hand both Kuroda and Tange never married and continued to study throughout their lives. At that time marriage meant giving up a woman's job. After becoming a housewife, she continued to study math by herself. Her philosophy was that studying math wasn't associated with getting a job or money. She studied math because she liked it (Murata, 1980).

Following Tohoku Teikoku Daigaku, Hokkaido Teikoku Daigaku's agriculture department in Sapporo City, Hokkaido decided to accept a female as a student for a special course which didn't offer a degree in 1918. *Jiji Newspaper* in September 23 said that a female student was born in Hokkaido Teikoku Daigaku. After graduating from Tokyo Joshi Kôtô Shihan Gakkô, Ms. Katô Setsuko was teaching at *kôtô jogakkô* in Sapporo (Hirano, 1977). Since she liked to study very much and wanted to learn gardening at the imperial university, she applied again and again. However, she received rejections twice because her ability was not enough to pass and study there. When she applied the third time, Hokkaido Teikoku Daigaku finally decided to accept her, saying, "Since she is too pretty, probably she will not be able to get a big success in the future. However, because she very much wants to study here, let's try accepting her." That charming and friendly girl soon became famous not only on campus but also at Sapporo. An innocent girl with a round face and bounding hair, she was liked by the other male students without discrimination though she had no time herself to pay attention to such a thing. She studied very hard in order to catch up with other students and she often studied without sleeping. Only her strong decision supported her. In 1921 she finished her agriculture study at Hokkaido Teikoku Daigaku (Hokkaido Daigaku, 1980).

Ms. Katô still continued to do research as an assistant at Hokkaido Teikoku Daigaku and as a researcher at the laboratory. In 1931 she received a Doctoral degree in science from Kyoto Teikoku Daigaku and after that she gave a lecture every year thereafter. After World War II she became a chief researcher in science for the Japanese government and made an effort to encourage more female doctoral students. As for her private life, she perfectly covered both her family and job, enjoying her private life with her family (Hokkaido Daigaku, 1980).

After being appointed to Kyoto Teikoku Daigaku as its president, Sawayanagi tried to open the school to female students. Though this issue was focused on by many public people, he could not do it successfully (Kageyama, 2000). The reasons why this school wouldn't accept female students were that there were no vacant seats for female students; it had enough male students, which was different from Tohoku Teikoku Daigaku's situation. In addition, because this school was established in Kyoto in 1897 by the Japanese government, it already had a history of male education and the professors in each department didn't agree with accepting the female students. However, in 1919 the rules for audit were extended to females and Kyoto Teikoku Daigaku's medical department accepted three female students to audit and the following year the economics department permitted four female students to audit their courses. The rules stated were: 1. This school permitted a student who didn't have a certification from Kyoto Teikoku Daigaku but wanted to sit in on one or two courses to audit them whenever there were vacant seats, 2. The student had to be older than 19 and pass an exam related to the subject one would study (Murata, 1980).

After promulgating a new rule in 1919 that would permit female students to audit courses there (Tokyo Teikoku Daigaku, 1932), in 1920 the department of literature at Tokyo Teikoku Daigaku accepted Ms. Uchida Toshiko, a teacher of Nihon Joshi Daiggakô, and 31 other female students to audit its courses. According to *The Yomiuri Shimbun* on September 12th, the oldest female student was Ms. Yoshimura Chizuko, 47 years old and the youngest ones were Ms. Hirano Chiyoko and Ms. Tsuruta Fusako, both 22 years old (Hirano, 1983). *Fujo Shimbun* reported this issue saying, "This is a big development for women. We'd pay our respects to farsighted professors considering current situations at this department. We hope that other departments will also accept female students not only as auditors but also as regular students in the near future" (*Fujo Shimbun*, 1920). In 1921 this department accepted 46 female students, and the departments of technology and of medicine each accepted a student to audit their courses (Nihon Joshi Daigaku Joshi Kyôiku Kenkyûsho, 1975). However, in 1928 this imperial university gave up the system of audit because of lack of funds from the damage of a big Kanto Earthquake in 1923 (Tokyo Daigaku 100 nenshi Henshû Iinkai, 1989).

The next imperial university to accept female students was Kyushu Teikoku Daigaku's law and literature department. This university had been established in Fukuoka Prefecture, Kyushu in 1903 as the second medical school of Kyoto Teikoku Daigaku. It was first known as Fukuoka Ika Daigaku (Fukuoka medical college) and became Kyushu Teikoku Daigaku independently in 1924. The chief of admissions, Mr. Minobe Tatsukichi, had this idea: If there were some girls graduating from *joshi kôtô shihan gakkô* and other *kôtô jogakkô* who wanted to study humanities and social sciences, this school would give them opportunities to study there in order to develop their higher education; however, this didn't mean the school permitted coeducation. The rules of entrance for Kyushu Teikoku Daigaku mentioned that this school would first accept the male applicants from high school and if there were still vacant seats, it would accept female students who graduated from *joshi kôtô shihan gakkô* or who had the same knowledge as they did (Kyushu Daigaku Sôritsu 50 shûnen Kinenkai, 1967). Under these rules the category 'female students' was clearly stated.

In 1925, Kyushu Teikoku Daigaku allowed two female students to enter this school. One was Ms. Orito Toyoko from Tokyo Joshi Daigaku and the other was Ms. Shirabe Sumako from Nara Joshi Kôtô Shihan Gakkô. Since this was a big event in that area, its local newspaper reported their score in order to prove that the female students' abilities were not inferior to those of other male students. Shirabe said that opening the university to us seemed to be equal to saving our lives. Three years later Orito became the first Bachelor of Economics and Shirabe the first Bachelor of Law in Japan. After the two female students gradated from this school, it accepted female students every year and the local newspaper used to report their situations (Kyushu Daigaku Sôritsu 50 shûnen Kinenkai, 1967).

Some public and private *senmongakkô* were promoted to colleges after 1918 when the Ordinance for Colleges was promulgated by the Japanese government, even though before 1918, only five imperial universities (Tokyo, Kyoto, Tohoku, Hokkaido and Kyushu) were permitted to offer college level courses. Japan came to have three other types of colleges such as national, public and private in addition to imperial universities because of this ordinance. National colleges were managed by the Japanese government,[7] public colleges were managed by prefectures or cities and private ones by juridical foundations whose purpose was only school management.

Tokyo Kôtô Shihan Gakkô and Hiroshima Kôtô Shihan Gakkô were promoted to national colleges as Tokyo Bunrika Daigaku and Hiroshima Bunrika Daigaku respectively and accepted female students in 1929. Tokyo Bunrika Daigaku allowed four female students, Ms. Shiomi Shimo, Ms. Akagi Shizuko, Ms. Katô Tokiwa and Ms. Nishida Matsuyo to study there. Hiroshima Bunrika Daigaku accepted a female student whose name was Ms. Tsujino Taeko. The following year, Ms. Fukushima Yuki and Ms. Kozuka Kiku were permitted to enter Hiroshima Bunrika Daigaku, and after the next year Ms. Yuasa Toshiko was accepted by Tokyo Bunrika Daigaku. By 1953, 95 female students graduated from Tokyo Bunrika Daigaku and 51 female students also did from Hiroshima Bunrika Daigaku (Murata, 1980).

Because it was still uncommon to have female students study in colleges where basically only male students attended, the female students needed strong determination and a lot of effort. A few students who graduated from these colleges remembered that they enjoyed studying there because they had very huge passions toward studying at college (Murata, 1980).

In addition to national colleges, in 1923 the private Dôshisha Daigaku serving male Japanese students accepted female students for special courses after being promoting to

---

[7] National colleges (universities) were turned into independent administrative entities in April, 2004. They gave up the government organizational framework and greatly expanded on the independence and autonomy of each university. However, they are still strongly connected with the government. The same can be said about public colleges (universities).

the college level in 1920 when it newly established a three-year high school and a three-year college. Originally, Dôshisha Senmongakkô was set up in 1875 by Mr. Niijima Jô whose ideas were based on Christianity. Niijima mentioned that a duty for every Christian was improving society. In order to do that, women's education was requisite. The rules associated with applicants in this school clearly mentioned the words 'female student,' asserting that those graduating from *senmongakkô* with a certificate could try the examination for this school. Dôshisha Daigaku also permitted female students graduated from the English course in Dôshisha women's *senmongakkô* to study there so that this school would be coeducational in the future. This was based on the Christian idea of educational equality (Dôshisha Shashi Shiryô Henshûsho, 1965).

Other private colleges such as Waseda Daigaku, Ryûkoku Daigaku (Yukawa, 1994), Keiôgijuku Daigaku (Keiôgijuku, 1968), Meiji Daigaku, Tôyô Daigaku, Hôsei Daigaku (Murata, 1980) and Nihon Daigaku (Nihon Joshi Daigaku Kyôiku Kenkyûsho, 1975) gradually accepted female students. However, the number of female students studying in these colleges were very few when considering the total enrollments. Their situations were still considered exceptions. Furthermore, female students studying in colleges were still not generally permitted by law in those days in Japan before World War II.

4) Rinji Kyôiku Kaigi (a Special Committee for Education) and Some Movements Associated with Women's Higher Education from around 1917 to during World War II

In 1917, around the same time when imperial universities began to accept female students, Rinji Kyôiku Kaigi (a special committee for education) was set up by the Ministry of Education in Japan (Japan, Rinji Kyôiku Kaigi, 1979a). Although it was abolished in May, 1919, it served effectively as an advisory body to the Prime Minister of Japan, examining Japanese education as a whole and aiming at correcting people's errant ways of thinking while pointing to new ways of developing the nation after World War I (Hashimoto, 1976). According to Imperial Ordinance 152 (Kaigo, 1960), Rinji Kyôiku Kaigi was invested with the authority to discuss and offer opinions about all the important educational issues the Prime Minister had assigned the Committee to examine. It could either explain its opinions about these important educational issues or suggest some new ideas related to them for his consideration. As organized, it had a president, a vice-president, both assigned by the Prime Minister, and 40 members assigned by the Ministry, which could add other members when needed. The president could pick specific members to explore any educational issue assigned. Included in the 40 members assigned were three privy advisors, some ministers, seven aristocrats, four members from the House of Representatives, four presidents from imperial universities and eight presidents from post secondary education institutes, including Naruse Jinzô Sawayanagi, President of the Imperial Educational Association. All of the members were men. The Ministry of Education did not offer opinions about those educational issues assigned to the Committee by the

Prime Minister in advance since opinions from Rinji Kyôiku Kaigi were thought to be quite authoritative in their impact. Every issue was examined by the Committee members and opinions to improve the issue were put forth. Later, these opinions were examined in a general meeting where the members, acting as a body, decided upon those final opinions which were going to be submitted to the Prime Minister (Kageyama, 2000b).

Sometime during 1912, when an increase in the number of young women coming to receive secondary and higher education (e.g., college level) for women was called for due to population growth and broader public perspectives, Issue No. 6 relating to women's education was included as one of the subjects the Committee examined. The main content of this issue had to do with improving the curriculum of *kôtô jogakkô* and women's higher education (Hashimoto, 1977). This issue was discussed at a general meeting on September 17, 1918, then at meetings held by some specific members on September 21, 25, 27 and 30 in 1918. At a general meeting on October 24, 1918, this issue was discussed again and final opinions decided which would be turned in to the Prime Minister in Japan. Regarding women's higher education examined at a general meeting in October 24 in 1918, there were three main opinions: 1. It was not necessary to establish a college for women since the present situation was adequate. It was enough to add a postgraduate course or a higher course in public secondary education institutions. Exceptional women who wanted to learn special skills were allowed to enter college such as Tohoku Teikoku Daigaku which had made a practice of accepting good female students. 2. Though the need for more attention to be paid to women's higher education was increasing year by year, there was no suitable institution in Japan to satisfy this growing need, and so some of the women have gone to study abroad to obtain higher education. For these reasons, the Japanese government should establish such a college system for women but these higher institutions should be separated from those of men because men and women were basically different (Japan, Rinji Kyôiku Kaigi, 1979b). This latter opinion was based on that of Mr. Naruse Jinzô, the president of Nihon Joshi Daigakkô. He said that women's education should be considered by following women's nature. He agreed with *'ryôsaikenbo'* and Japanese systems based on families. The happiest situation for women was marrying and taking care of their children to develop the country. In order to obtain this situation, women needed a higher education which was different from that of men. Though he didn't deny coeducation, it was inconvenient to develop women's talent because of certain aspects related to public morals. Women's college should aim at training perfect women who had both academic knowledge and a good personality as women (Kaigo, 1960). 3. Higher education seemed to give women physical disadvantages. A lot of study and pressure from higher education prevented women from building up physical strength. It meant that the number of women dying would increase and that of delivering children would decrease. Children were most important for the nation. Therefore, even adding a postgraduate course or higher course in public secondary institutions should not be permitted. This third opinion came from Mr. Yamakawa, the president of Tokyo Teikoku Daigaku, and included the meaning that women didn't need higher education because it kept them from pursuing their essential job of reproducing the nation's descendants. Such women as wanted to study at an imperial university were strange and lacked women's nature. As a result, the first opinion was decided on at the general meeting and turned in to the Prime Minister (Kageyama, 2000b). In 1920, a higher course for two or three years was added in the public secondary education institutions. This higher course consisted of general education which was different from the education offered at *senmongakkô,* whose purpose was mainly focused on vocational education. Because the basic Japanese governmental way of thinking about women's duty was doing domestic work and taking care of children for the nation without having an 'outside' job, there were no national *senmongakkô* for women at that time. Only Tokyo Joshi Kôtô Shihan Gakkô and Nara Joshi Kôtô Shihan Gakkô were managed by the Government. For this reason, even if a woman graduated from this higher course of instruction, she couldn't obtain official qualification such as a teacher's certification which would be associated with such an 'outside' job.

In addition to Rinji Kyôiku Kaigi, there were other movements related to women's higher education because of an increasing sense of democratic ideas coming in from the outside about women's rights and self-consciousness, symbolized by women's suffrage which was obtained one by one in Western countries after World War I. Though some imperial universities and colleges began to open their gates to female students, the number of these was still very few and higher education was not being spread to include ordinary women as yet. Because there was no female high school, the preparatory school for college, women were actually shut out from college education. Moreover, national *senmongakkô* were not accepting female students because of each school's rule, except for Tokyo Ongaku Senmongakkô[8], although female applicants graduating from *kôtô jogakkô* were permitted by law to apply. Under such circumstances, there was much discussion about this issue, to 'Open male colleges to female students!' For example, in one newspaper, some people were talking about whether male colleges, high schools and *sen-*

---

[8] It is a music school.

mongakkô should be open to female students. The president of Waseda Daigaku, Mr. Hiranuma, said that male colleges and *senmongakkô* should accept female students who had demonstrated enough ability to study there. As for college education, female students should be accepted not only as students to audit some courses but also as regular students who could obtain their degrees. Regarding this issue when associated with high school, male high schools should open their doors to female students or else female high schools should be newly established. A professor of Tokyo Gaikokugo Gakkô (Tokyo special school of foreign languages), Mr. Katayama, agreed with Hiranuma's opinion, adding that if male high schools were open to female students, the schools needed to consider some plans related to public morals for adolescences. On the other hand, Professor Tsuboi of Tokyo Teikoku Daigaku insisted that because men and women were different physically and psychologically, they should not study together. If needed, female colleges and high schools should be established. (In 1920, Tokyo Teikoku Daigaku would accept female students to audit some courses.) He also didn't agree with the opinion that male *senmongakkô* should be open to female students (*Fujo Shimbun*, 1919, May 23).

The President of Fujo Newspaper Pubishing Company, Mr. Fukushima, wrote articles to persuade ordinary people to take part in his plan to submit a petition related to improving women's education to the Japanese government through the *Fujo shimbun* (*Fujo Shimbun*, 1919, November 30). He presented a clear picture for that time showing that there were no female colleges, high schools and national *senmongakkô* and he tried to gather signatures from people who agreed with his opinions. In 1920, Fukushima and about 2000 other people submitted to Government a petition requiring the opening of male *senmongakkô* and high schools to female students or newly establishing female *senmongakkô* and high schools because of the rapid increase in the number of women who wanted to enjoy higher education (Yukawa, 1997). What's more, in 1925 and 1926, similar petitions were submitted by other groups, one being a female student union whose purpose was to solve those problems arising from unequal educational opportunities (Hashimoto, 1976). In 1928, Mr. Fukushima and another 564 people submitted a petition to establish a women's college to prepare teachers for higher courses in public *kôtô jogakkô* (Yukawa, 1997).

Among presidents of *kôtô jogakkô,* there was the idea that those higher courses which had been added to public *kôtô jogakkô* should themselves be upgraded to female high schools thus making them preparatory schools for colleges. Opinions arose that opening male high schools to female students would cause new problems to arise associated with public morals about adolescence and that establishing female high schools would cause huge new expenses (Takahashi, 1983). However, these concerns as well as the petitions submitted by the people never came to fruition because of the Japanese government's disagreements.

Issues related to coeducation were also focused on by individual people in those days. After 1918 when the Ordinance for Colleges was promulgated by the Japanese government, private *senmongakkô* Keiôgijuku and Waseda were upgraded in official status to colleges. These schools were planning to change their male policy to coeducation and accept female students under the same conditions as male students. In 1919, Keiôgijuku Daigaku applied to the Ministry of Education in Japan to change its school ordinance to read that its high school would accept female students. However, the Ministry of Education didn't agree to this because there was no school law that permitted female students to be accepted in high schools. Waseda Daigaku also was not permitted to change its admission policy to coeducation (*Fujo Shimbun*, 1920, January 18). The president of Waseda Daigaku, Mr. Hiranuma said that coeducation was going to be the foundation for building up a civilization more geared to 20th century standards. In addition, the president of Keiôgijuku Daigaku, Mr. Kamata, mentioned that the Japanese nation needed to consider the happiness of human beings by aiming at training perfect men and women and by offering higher education to women who were to his mind equal to men in consideration (Yukawa, 1994).

Mr. Sawayanagi introduced his opinion that higher education should be coeducational because there was nothing different in the study of medicine by men or women. Women had to learn the same techniques men used. Furthermore, coeducation didn't have to spend a lot of new expenses like newly establishing women's higher institutions (Sawayanagi, 1919, March 14). Mr. Fukushima, the president of Fujo Newspaper Publishing Company agreed with Sawayanagi's opinion saying that, although people sometimes suggested that secondary education should be offered in separate schools if we could solve the issue of public morals, the planners didn't need to worry about it. Whenever there are a lot of male and female students in a room, they would naturally watch their behavior toward each other. What's more, since this world was organized by men and women, it would be unnatural for them to have education separately. Education in separate schools might produce unbalanced human beings rather than well rounded ones (Fukushima, 1920, April 4).

According to Ms. Yosano Akiko, a famous writer at that time, people should accept democracy and the idea of equality between men and women by getting rid of the conservative ideas of Confucianism. Every level of education should be coeducational and women should be given the same opportunities for education and vocations that men had (Kageyama, 2000b).

Ms. Koizumi Ikuko, a pioneer of coeducation having received her M.A. degree in the US after finishing Tokyo Joshi Kôtô Shihan Gakkô, pointed out that coeducation was one of the ways to reach a new and ideal culture of cooperation between men and women, and furthermore, that coeducation itself was the new culture. All disharmony in society was based on disharmony between men and women and we needed cooperation between them in order to develop society. If education was needed to contribute to a better society, then coeducation was the principle to be followed. For these reasons, schools should be coeducational and female high schools, colleges and *senmongakkô* didn't need to be established (Koizumi, 1933).

On the other hand, there were some people who insisted on separate schools. According to Mr. Tago Kazutomi, Secretary of Home Affairs, while equality of men and women was based on their personality, actually, their natures were different. Coexistence between men and women was meaningful for developing society because their natures were different. As an example, after an ordinance promulgated by men is examined by intellectual women, we might have a better ordinance. Since their ways of thinking are different due to different natures, women's might find better points which men wouldn't necessarily find. For these reasons, men and women should study in separate schools in order to develop their different natures (Tago, 1919, April. 4).

The opinion of Naruse Jinzô, the president of Nihon Joshi Daigakkô, was similar to that of Tago. He also focused on women's education based on women's nature. Furthermore, he presented his ideal of a women's college that was different from male and female colleges in Western countries. It was a unique Japanese institution including new elements from Western countries combined with traditional elements in Eastern countries. He focused on educating well-rounded people emphasizing good personalities, and established three courses such as home economics, medicine and religion to accomplish this goal. Home economics related to science offered these students skills which would contribute to their building perfect families with complete freedoms to raise children who would support the nation in the future. Medicine helped the students obtain not only what was associated with keeping their bodies healthy but also developing their spirits of affection and sacrifice. Religion included literature, education, art, music and the like, all of which contributed to training their ethics, values and emotions (Tago, 1919, April 4).

After Naruse's ideas about the women's college were reported in *Fujo Shimbun* in 1919, private women's *senmongakkô* began to prepare for raising their schools up to be women's colleges. Kobe Jogakuin in 1919, Tokyo Joshi Daigaku in 1922 and Joshi Eigaku Juku in 1928 set up college departments so that their systems were the same as the men's college. Though in 1926, Nihon Joshi Daigakkô applied to the Ministry of Education for permission to establish a women's college, it was not granted (Yukawa, 2001).

Both Tokyo and Nara Joshi Kôtô Shihan Gakkô, as well as private female *senmongakkô* all started movements to elevate their schools to be women's colleges (Takahashi, 1989). *Shihan kyôiku kaizô dômei* (a union to improve normal schools' education), established by those interested in improving normal schools, decided to make an effort to promote *joshi kôtô shihan gakkô* to colleges at a meeting in 1923. After that, Tokyo Joshi Kôtô Shihan Gakkô and Nara Joshi Kôtô Shihan Gakkô began movements to promote their schools to colleges cooperatively (Ochanomizu Joshi Daigaku 100 nenshi Kankô Iinkai, 1984). Their statements were: 1. Though both Tokyo

Kôtô Shihan Gakkô and Hiroshima Kôtô Shihan Gakkô were already raised to college level as Tokyo Bunrika Daigaku and Hiroshima Bunrika Daigaku respectively in 1923, why weren't women's normal schools permitted to elevate themselves? 2. Women's normal colleges were needed because there were no institutions to train teachers for those higher courses added in public secondary education institutes. 3. It was the time to set up women's normal colleges for female students who wanted to have higher education. 4. We needed women's normal colleges whose characters were different from those of men's normal colleges in order to develop women's own natures (Tokyo Joshi Kôtô Shihan Gakkô Henshû, 1934).

In 1927, Tokyo Kôtô Shihan Gakkô's alumna association established Sakuraiinkai in order to unite these movements saying, "Men and women were equal under education. If there were colleges for men, there should be colleges for women." In 1930, the Association asked the Japanese government to establish a women's college which had a literature department, science department, home economics department and physical education department. What's more, it started movements for improving various affairs related to normal schools with other unions (Ochanomizu Joshi Daigaku 100 nenshi Kankô Iinkai, 1984).

In 1937, Kyôiku Shingikai (a committee for discussing educational issues) was set up as an advisory body for the Prime Minister in Japan though it was abolished in 1942. After many movements associated with elevating women's higher normal schools, Kyôiku Shingikai finally decided on those opinions to submit to the prime minister in a general meeting on September 19, 1940. The opinions were to establish women's high schools whose curriculum content was the same as that of men, and women's colleges with a home economics department. The reason why they were permitted to establish women's high schools and colleges was the outbreak of war between China and Japan, which started in 1931. War between them in 1937 grew stuck and no one knew when or how the war was going to finish. For this reason, the Japanese government needed more and more women to perform men's roles. However, education for developing women's own natures was still emphasized (Tachi, 1978).

After the outbreak of World War II, Mr. Matsuura, a member of Kyôiku Shingikai, organized the Ordinance for Women's College. It designated that: 1. A college which accepted only women must be called a women's college. 2. It would include a literature department and a science department. 3. An applicant should have graduated from a girls' high school, a higher course in a secondary education institution, or be a student who had the same knowledge those others would have. 4. The college could set up a high school whose curriculum level would be the same as that of the higher courses in secondary education institutions. 5. The high school addition, to run three years, would accept a student from *kôtô jogakkô* or a student who had the same knowledge as the student from *kôtô jogakkô*. 6. The content of the curriculum and so forth in the high school addition should follow those of the higher course in secondary education institutions. 7. Rules for the women's college should follow those of men's colleges with some exceptions (Ochanomizu Joshi Daigaku 100 nenshi Kankô Iinkai, 1984). However, because it was in the middle of World War II, the emergency situation in Japan could not help but stop all these plans, and nothing came of them until after World War II.

Because during World War II education received a lot of influence from Japanese militarism, people's meetings and freedom of speech, education and thought were prohibited. The Japanese government emphasized traditional Japanese ways of thinking and gave up accepting Western ideas. English education in Japan was severely damaged. After the start of World War II, English became an enemy's language; it changed from a required subject to an elective one. Finally, teaching and learning were entirely abolished and people tried not to use English in their daily conversations (Tsuda Juku Daigaku, 1960).

The Japanese government ordered schools to have earlier graduations in 1941. Following this order, Kyôritsu Joshi Gakuen allowed their students to graduate from school three months earlier than expected in 1941 and six months earlier in 1942 (Takase, 1956). At the same time *kôtô jogakkô,* normally five years became four years in length and the four-year *senmongakkô* were reduced to three years to finish (Tsuda Juku Daigaku, 1960).

Mobilizing students into work associated with the war effort began in 1939 and students had to take part in works of agriculture, air defense facilities and munitions supply as workers. After World War II began, this student mobilization was more emphasized and in 1943, students had to work three months a year; in 1944, four months a year. On August 23, 1944, the Japanese government promulgated the Ordinance of Women's Volunteer Corps and encouraged women to take part in work related to the war effort. Many female students in secondary and post secondary institutions stayed in factories to make munitions. During their stay, they had to keep to strict rules. For example, all letters to them were checked and they were not allowed to go home even if one of the members of their families died. Going outside freely was prohibited and it was not easy to see their families without being considered a spy (Nara Joshi Daigaku 60 nenshi Henshû Iinkai, 1970). Male students were called up to fight in battlefields because of a growing lack of army personnel. They had no rights to avoid serving in the war. If they refused or even complained, they went to jail. Many young male college and *senmongakkô* students went to the battlefields saying that they were going to do their best for their country even if they died. On March 18, 1945, the Japanese government decided to stop all education except for elementary students. The emerging situation in Japan did not allow people to study easily.

Desperate results were expected. A lot of bombs from US air force machines were dropped all over Japan every day like showers. After Germany, one of Japan's allies, accepted unconditional surrender on June 23, 1945, Okinawa's defense forces were destroyed. Finally, atomic bombs were dropped on Hiroshima on August 6 and Nagasaki on August 9, 1945. Japan accepted the Potsdam Declaration, ending the war with the US and its allies on August 15, 1945. During the war, women were required to work for the country as well as men while the Japanese government insisted that they keep unequal, traditional education policies. However, these systems were abolished at a stroke after defeat because of the American occupation's general policy emphasizing democracy.

5) Occupations

When paying attention to the occupational situations of national normal schools at the highest level (e.g., Tokyo Joshi Kôtô Shihan Gakkô and Nara Joshi Kôtô Sihan Gakkô) from 1910 to 1942, we can see that 94% of all students in both schools received jobs each year (Table 2). Teaching positions included teaching at Joshi Kôtô Shihan Gakkô (both Tokyo and Nara), normal schools for training elementary school teachers, *kôtô jogakkô* and other schools, and also further education including courses in their own schools or national colleges after 1913 in order to study more.

Regarding Tokyo Joshi Kôtô Shihan Gakkô, 99% of the students in 1910, 92% in 1920, 86% in 1930, 97% in 1940 and 96% in 1942 found teaching positions. Those students whose disposition was unknown amounted to only 1% in 1910, 7% in 1920, 12% in 1930, 1.9% in 1940 and 2.8% in 1942. Those going for further education in Japan were 1% or 2% of all students where listed. In the case of Nara Joshi Kôtô Shihan Gakkô, 100% of the students found jobs in 1920, 84% in 1930, 97% in 1940 and 94% in 1942. In 1930, 1.5 % had no job, 1% in 1940, while those in 1942 who had not decided amounted to 6.1%. Those going into further education in Japan here were also 1% or 2% of those listed.

The average percentage of the students getting jobs during these 32 years in both schools was 94%, which was a very good result. According to these sources, we can see there were no big changes concerning teaching positions between 1910 to 1940 and 1942 during World War II. One of the reasons for recording a lower percentage of employment in graduates of both schools after 1930 seems to have been the influence of the Japanese recession which occurred after a brief period of prosperity following World War I and the

Table 2 : Students' occupational situations after their graduation

Table 2-a Tokyo Joshi Kôtô Shihan Gakkô

	teaching positions	further education	undecided	those who died	total
1910	90(99%)	0	1(1%)	0	91(100%)
1920	83(92%)	0	7(7%)	0	90(100%)
1930	85(86%)	2(2%)	12(12%)	0	99(100%)
1940	100(97%)	1(1%)	2(1.9%)	0	103(100%)
1942	243(96%)	2(0.8%)	7(1.9%)	0	252(100%)
average%	94%	0.76%	4.9%	0%	100%

Table 2-b Nara Joshi Kôtô Shihan Gakkô

	teaching positions	further education	undecided	those who died	total
1920	57(100%)	0	0	0	57(100%)
1930	79(84%)	1(1%)	14(1.5%)	0	94(100%)
1940	87(97%)	2(2.2%)	1(1%)	0	90(100%)
1942	77(94%)	0	5(6.1%)	0	82(100%)
average%	94%	0.8%	2.15%	0%	100%

Sources: *Monbushô Nenpô* 38, 48, 58, 68 and 70.

world depression which started in America in 1929.

Concerning women's *senmongakkô*, the number of graduates from 1904 to 1921 at Nihon Joshi Daigakkô was 2,047 while those remaining in 1921 were 1,785; the number 2,047 including those who died and those abroad. The graduates engaged in occupations were 360 out of 1,785 and this rate was 20% of all. The education field accepted 62% out of 360 and their positions included professors at Nihon Joshi Daigakkô, advisors of dormitories, teachers and presidents of *kôtô jogakkô*, teachers and presidents of kindergartens, and private tutors. Research and social work accepted 31% and they were students who had further education in schools and people working in associations related to women and children, cooperative societies, journals and libraries. The remaining 7% had occupations as medical doctors, office workers and jobs in royal families. It should be understood that 74 out of the 360 or 21% of all were housewives too. What's more, there were 648 graduates from 1913 to 1928 in Nihon Joshi Daigakkô and 46% of them were employed after their graduation (Ryôsawa, 1981). According to the survey by the Japanese government, in 1927 the total number of female students graduating from 10 *senmongakkô* was 1,206 and 287 students out of 1,206 obtained jobs. This was 23.8% of all (Chûô Shokugyô Shôkai Jimukyoku, 1937).

In 1928, the Japanese government reported the rate of general *senmongakkô* women receiving jobs was 20.2% while 50.8% of the women had no job related occupations. However, 77% of women from medical schools were engaged in jobs while only 12.8% of them had no jobs (Table 3). At that time a teaching position was the easiest thing for women to obtain but gradually, some began to be engaged in the posi-

Table 3 : Students' situations after graduation in 1928

	people getting a job	owning a business	further education	no job	others	total	actual number
senmongakkô (general)	20.2%	0	4.1%	50.8%	24.9%	100%	1,448
senmongakkô (medicine)	77%	9.1%	1.1%	12.8%	0	100%	187

Table 4 : Occupations in 1928

	public official	educational institution	company	hospital	mass media	others	total
senmongakkô (general)	0.7%	90.5%	1.7%	0.3%	1.00%	5.8%	293 (100%)
senmongakkô (medicine)	0	4.2%	0	85.4%	0	10.4%	144 (100%)

Sources: *Kyôiku Shakaigaku Kenkyû* V. 33, 1978.

tions of journalist, secretary, public official, office worker and librarian (Table 4).

Regarding their salaries in the first month, in 1930 ($1 = ¥2) medical section salaries were 110 yen (about 55 dollars, the highest salary) and 80 yen (about 40 dollars, the average) (Amano, 1978). Women were working mainly at hospitals and medical rooms, department stores, banks and factories. If running her own clinic with a good reputation, she could earn 400 or 500 yen (about 200 to 250 dollars) (Tokyo Joshi Shûshoku Shidôkai, 1994). Salaries in educational fields ranged from 90 yen (about 45 dollars, the highest) to 75 yen (about 37 dollars and 50 cents, the average) in terms of higher education (Amano, 1978). The salary for elementary school teachers was about 40 yen (about 20 dollars) and that for secondary education teachers was about 50 yen (about 25 dollars). They also had a 20 yen (about 10 dollar) to 60 yen (about 30 dollars) bonus a year after five years and a pension after retirement based on how long they worked. The salary of the office worker was 20 to 30 yen and they worked at various places such as government offices, banks, companies and department stores. As for journalists, they earned 25 yen to 50 yen a month (Tokyo Joshi Shûshoku Shidôkai, 1994). Women's salaries were about 70%–80% of men's salaries in each job.

The rates of *senmongakkô* women obtaining jobs between 1930 and 1934 were 25% in 1930, 21.8% in 1931, 25.6% in 1932, 28.8% in 1933 and 30.1% in 1934 (Chûo Shokugyô Shôkai Jimukyoku, 1935). In 1936, the Japanese government reported the job situations of female students who graduated from *senmongakkô* in Table 5. This information was obtained from 42 female *senmongakkô* that the Ministry of Education in Japan had picked out. General *senmongakkô* referred to female students graduating from literature, home economics, law and business courses while medical *senmongakkô* graduated female students from medical, pharmacological and dentistry courses. Table 5 also included students who engaged in domestic work at home. When it came to general *senmongakkô*, the number of students graduating from those schools was 2,737 while the number of those getting jobs was 627 and owning their own businesses was 8. This was 23.2% of all while others were 62.6% of all. The number of going for further education was 5.6% and those with no job was 8.6%. In the case of medical *senmongakkô*, the number of the students finishing schools was 896 and those obtaining jobs was 543. The rate of getting jobs was 64.5% after adding those owning their business, 32. The numbers of others, those going for further education, and those with no job were 12.3%, 21.1% and 2.1%, respectively. According to this data, we can see that medical *senmongakkô* contributed more to women's getting jobs than the general ones. Table 6 presents what occupations students obtained after their graduations by focusing on only 627 students in general *senmongakkô* and 543 in medical ones as salaried women. 76.9% in general *senmongakkô* worked in schools while 66% in medical ones got jobs in medical fields (though this was reasonable). The occupations which had the second largest rates of employment were in industry (10.7%) from general *senmongakkô,* and in schools (13.2%) from the medical *senmongakkô.*

Here we focus on some general *senmongakkô* which were origins of women's higher education in those days. In Table 7 and 8 they were Nihon Joshi Daigakkô, Joshi Eigaku Juku,

Table 5 : Students' situations after graduation in 1936

	getting Job	owning a business	further education	no job	others	the number of students graduating
general senmongakkô	627 22.9%	8 0.3%	153 5.6%	236 8.6%	1713 62.6%	2,737 100%
medical senmongakkô	543 61%	32 3.5%	190 21.1%	20 2.1%	111 12.3%	896 100%

Table 6 : Occupations

	in government	in school	in medical fields	in industry	others	total
general senmongakkô	16 2.6%	482 76.9%	19 3%	67 10.7%	43 6.8%	627 100%
medical senmongakkô	27 4.8%	72 13.2%	357 66%	56 10.3%	31 5.7%	543 100%

Source: *Chishiki Kaikyû Shûshoku ni Kansuru Shiryô*, 1937.

Kobe Jogakuin, Tokyo Joshi Daigaku, Jissen Joshi Gakuen, Kyôritsu Joshi Gakuen and Joshi Bijutsu Gakkô. The Japanese government reported the students' situations after their graduations in 1942 from those schools. The average rate of getting jobs in those schools in 1942 was 36.4%. Joshi Bijutsu Gakkô had the highest rate of 72% and the lowest rate was 10% which was Kobe Jogakuin. Others in the table presented the students engaging in domestic work in their houses. There were some students who went on to further education. Although there were some differences between the schools in terms of the rate of getting jobs, all of the students getting jobs in those schools found them in government, teaching, and banks. This seemed to be a special situation for those schools. When looking at Table 8, we can see that teaching was the most popular among the students. In Joshi Bijutsu Gakkô, all students getting jobs that year were engaged in teaching positions while even the students in Tokyo Joshi Daigaku, whose rate was the lowest, 51%, obtained teaching positions. The percentage of students' working in government and banks looks almost the same:

Finally, this data concludes that women's main jobs at that time were teachers and medical workers from medical doctors to pharmacists, and the number of students who were engaged in jobs from two *joshi kôtô shihangakkô* and medical *senmongakkô* was much more than that of those from general *senmongakkô*. The teaching position was also popular

Table 7 : Students' situations after graduation in some general senmongakkô in 1942

	the number getting jobs	further education	unknown	those who died	others	total	the rate of getting jobs
Nihon Joishi Daigakkô	63	23	2	2	242	332	19%
Joshi Eigaku Juku	42	7	0	0	38	87	48%
Kobe Jogakuin	13	5	0	1	107	126	10%
Tokyo Joshi Daigaku	47	3	0	0	84	134	35%
Jissen Joshi Gakuen	194	5	0	1	256	456	43%
Kyôritsu Joshi Gakuen	170	161	0	5	220	556	31%
Joshi Bijutsu Gakkô	67	0	0	0	26	93	72%

Table 8 : Occupations in some general senmongakkô in 1942

	in government	teaching	in banks	total
Nihon Joshi Daigakkô	11 / 17%	43 / 68%	9 / 15%	63 / 100%
Joshi Eigaku Juku	8 / 19%	28 / 67%	6 / 14%	42 / 100%
Kobe Jogakuin	1 / 8%	9 / 69%	3 / 23%	13 / 100%
Tokyo Joshi Daigaku	14 / 30%	24 / 51%	9 / 19%	47 / 100%
Jissen Joshi Gakuen	9 / 5%	160 / 82%	25 / 13%	194 / 100%
Kyôritsu Joshi Gakuen	3 / 2%	167 / 98%	0	170 / 100%
Joshi Bijutsu Gakkô	0	67 / 100%	0	67 / 100%

Source: *Monbushô Nenpô* 70.

among the students in general *senmongakkô* and the rate of getting this job was the highest there. Generally speaking, women's higher normal schools and medical *senmongakkô* focused on vocational education while most of the general *senmongakkô* emphasized liberal arts and discipline, including the idea of becoming a good wife and wise mother, which didn't very much relate to specific occupations. This tendency was from the Japanese government's idea that women should stay at home, manage domestic affairs and take care of their children without having outside jobs in order to develop the nation. Because the number of higher normal schools and medical *senmongakkô* was much less than that of general *senmongakkô*, the rate of getting jobs on the whole was not high. In addition, since most of the students in *senmongakkô* were from the middle and upper classes and didn't have to be engaged in occupations to make their living, the number getting jobs was small. For this reason, the numbers of others in the tables were high because they performed domestic work at home. In other words, graduating from *senmongakkô* symbolized their high social status. Even though some women obtained jobs after finishing *senmongakkô*, most of them quit their jobs after marriage. The last reason there were not many jobs for women having higher education at that time was because the Japanese nation didn't see the need then for such women's work.

CHAPTER II

Women's Higher Education and Social Position after World War II in Japan

1) Education Reform after World War II and the American Occupation

The Potsdam Declaration, which was issued on July 27, 1945 after Germany's surrender, proposed removing militarism in Japan, making Japanese territories smaller and respecting human rights by emphasizing democracy. It also included that Japan would be occupied by America until completing the issues described above. Japan accepted this declaration and promised to follow the advice from the Supreme Command for the Allied Powers (SCAP) to give up the authority of both the Japanese Emperor and Japanese government. Japan also declared that new Japanese political forms would be decided on based on people's free opinions (Ienaga, 1977).

After World War II the condition of Japanese education was terrible and completely ineffective. Many children couldn't study because their schools were destroyed by the war. The Japanese military occupied top positions in education and controlled everything. Very few books were available. Japan didn't have enough teachers to begin with, and teachers having ideas of democracy were kept from teaching by the military police. On August 15, 1945, World War II ended when Japan accepted unconditional surrender. During World War II, Japan lost 3,100,000 people and it was overwhelming to think about. Under such conditions, it was very difficult for Japan by itself to reform its education (Suzuki, 1983).

In September, 1945, General Douglas MacArthur, Supreme Commander for the Allied Powers, arrived in Japan in order to carry out the Allies' policies, including removing militarism, establishing democracy and respecting human rights. After arriving in Japan, he recognized the necessity for educational reform as he criticized the anti-democratic educational situation in Japan. MacArthur (1964, p.311)mentioned:

> The educational system when I arrived in Japan gave me deep concern. The Japanese practiced central control over the schools. There was no such thing as a local school board or superintendent. A ministry of education in Tokyo bought standard textbooks in everything, and distributed them throughout the country. These textbooks were filled with militaristic and anti-America items, and all was under the control of Tokyo. As a matter of fact, up until the time of the occupation, the schools, newspapers, theater, radio, and motion pictures were all part of an official propaganda machine, and can be said to have existed for the purpose of "thought control" rather than for their own intrinsic purpose.

MacAthur did not ignore women's education. On October 11, 1945 he required the Japanese government to draw up a new constitution based on democracy and five special reforms including equality between men and women and a democratic school education from bottom to top. On December 4 of the same year, Mr. Ômura, the Vice Minister of Education in Japan at that time, promulgated a new outline for women's education. There were three elements to it: policy, main points to be explored and dispositions. 1. Policy: The Japanese government would reform women's education by emphasizing equal opportunity and content of education between men and women in order to promote mutual understanding between them. 2. Main points to be explored: For the present, the new Japanese government tried to lift the levels of women's higher and secondary education up to the same level as men's education in order to establish coeducation procedures. 3. Dispositions: a. establish women's colleges and enforce coeducation, b. seriously consider establishing high schools for girls and offer the same educational courses both to boys and girls, and c. open lectures in *senmongakkô* and colleges to women. The important thing the Japanese government wanted to do throughout was to improve women's education by removing unequal educational conditions including coeducation in colleges (Katayama, 1984).

By the end of 1945, Supreme Command for the Allied Powers (SCAP) eliminated old Japanese policies containing militarism and ultra-nationalism one by one, banished those teachers who cooperated with the war, separated education from religious institutions, and stopped classes teaching moral discipline and Japanese history encouraging the War in their favor (Katayama, 1984). On January 4, 1946 MacArthur asked through the appropriate channels in America to send Japan an education mission, which would stay in Japan about one month, to create the needed educational reforms, there being no educational specialist in the Education Division of the Civil Information and Education Section (CIE) in SCAP. He wanted this mission to examine four things: 1. democratic education in Japan, 2. psychological aspects toward new education in Japan, 3. re-organization of Japanese educational public administration, and 4. higher education for rebuilding the Japanese nation (Nishi, 1983). After receiving the order from MacArthur, the Department of War sent this message to the Department of State to choose educational advisors who would go to Japan. After several exchanges between CIE and the Department of State, 27 American educational specialists were picked out, including Dr. George D. Stoddard, chairman of the group, State Commissioner of Education in New York and President-elect of the University of Illinois (Tsuchimochi, 1993). Fourteen members of the mission were associated with universities, five others from educational administrations, four from associations related to education and labor, and four from the federal government. The 19 people from universities and educational administrations came from all over the U.S. (Suzuki, 1983). Because SCAP also ordered the Japanese government to produce a committee composed of Japanese educators to cooperate with the American mission, the Ministry of Education[9] in Japan gathered 29 educators including Mr. Nanbara, President of Tokyo Teikoku Daigaku. Most of the members of this committee were presidents or professors of universities, colleges and *senmongakkô* (Igasaki & Yoshihara, 1975).

In 1946, 27 members of the first American mission arrived at Japan on March 5 and 6. On March 8, the Ministry of Education in Japan and the Japanese education committee had the first meeting with the American mission. At that time Mr. Abe, the Minister of Education, mentioned, "To tell the truth, we can't help feeling pressure from America, a victorious country. We believe that with justice and truth the American education mission would give us good advice and opportunities to correct defects in Japanese education by re-

---

[9] The Ministry of Education changed its name to the Ministry of Education, Culture, Sports, Science and Technology in 2001.

moving bad customs and disadvantageous points. We would appreciate it if you would consider respecting Japanese culture and nationality which has had a long history without insisting on points of view about America as a victorious country" while he explained the remorse Japan had over the mistakes of World War II and the needed American aid to contribute towards improving Japanese education. In return, Dr. G. D. Stoddard, chairman of the American education mission said, "We are here not to criticize Japan and Japanese people but to improve Japanese education by removing bad elements and helping good points so that they would be better. If we can succeed in improving Japanese education with the Japanese education committee, it will be great usefulness both for Japan and for America" (Igasaki & Yoshihara, 1975). Japanese educational reform immediately began to be carried out by the American education mission, carefully considering the Japanese committee's point of view by keeping a good relationship between American and Japanese intentions.

The members of CIE also gathered information about Japanese education and gave lectures to the mission to help them understand Japanese educational situations more thoroughly even though the mission already had some ideas about it in America. On March 14, 1946, Capt. Eileen Donovan, who took charge of women's education, gave a lecture to the mission. She had graduated from normal school in Boston, had had experiences of teaching history and economics in middle school and had worked for the Federal government (Ito, 1990). She explained that most of the women in Japan didn't have enough fundamental knowledge to help rebuild the nation because the formal level of women's education in Japan was very low. The duty of Japanese women was obedience to their parents, their husband and their sons, emphasizing *ryôsaikenbo*. The level of girls' education at the secondary level was much lower than that of boys, and there was little opportunity for women to have a college education with very few exceptions. Moreover, there was no women's college. Although in December 1945, the Japanese government promulgated the new outline for women's education, there was no specialist in their government for women's education. Lastly, she emphasized the necessity of a change in women's attitudes toward their social positions, Japanese women's recognition of their natures and women's right to know (Suzuki, 1983).

After understanding Japanese educational situations from the lectures and the information gathered by CIE, the American education mission began to get in touch with the Japanese committee positively and important issues were decided on based on discussion between the two. Finally, on March 31, 1946, Dr. G. D. Stoddard, chairman of the mission, submitted the Report of the United States Education Mission to Japan to SCAP (Nakajima, 1970).

The report of the United States Education Mission to Japan included an introduction and a five-page foreword at the beginning and was organized into six parts: 1. the purpose of Japanese education and its contents, 2. reforming of Japanese language, 3. educational administration of elementary and secondary level, 4. education about the teacher and one's class, 5. adult education, and 6. higher education. The report described general advice for reforming Japanese education focusing on the importance of individual value and dignity and freedom of education and research. It also presented reforms of curriculum, school system, financial administration, teacher's education with much thinking about specialization, textbooks about ethics, history, geography, health education, physical education and Japanese language, all the while introducing the 6–3–3–4 single education system (nine-year obligatory education), coeducation, decentralization, the system of the board of education, liberal arts in higher education and the importance of increasing the number of public libraries for adult education (Suzuki, 1983). These recommendations were very useful for reforming the Japanese education system at that time and most of them were carried out.

Because the mission recognized the traditional educational discrimination between men and women based on gender, the report said in its introduction and foreword that the Japanese people should respect women's elevated social position as a whole in this new educational system for Japan with its equal opportunities in education for men and women which would contribute to a system far better than the old one currently in practice (Igasaki & Yoshihara, 1975). Chapter 1, the purpose of Japanese education and its contents, discussed the importance of women's education by saying that a good wife and wise mother was never encouraged by circumstances which didn't offer enough real knowledge to round out one's experience. This meant that the importance of women's awaking in order to build up a democratic society in some way denied the idea of a good wife and wise mother by itself. Formal education took the priority in helping women understand these new concepts. Chapter 3, educational administration in elementary and secondary levels, pointed out that this education should have the same curriculum in the same classrooms based on the idea of equal opportunities in education. Chapter 6, higher education, should become more of an opportunity for the masses and not just for a privileged few. It criticized old Japanese educational systems that held a big gap between higher education for a small number of people and ordinary education for others, suggesting that higher education needed to be open for everyone, women as well as men, to aspire to. The most important thing that Japan had to now do, was to train young men and women in higher education and to produce talented young people who would support the nation in the future economically, politically and culturally in order to recover from the miserable situation Japan found itself in because of its defeat from World War II (Murata, 1980). For this reason, women who were ready for higher education should be allowed to have it immediately (Nakajima, 1970).

The first American education mission required female expertise in order to improve women's higher education in Japan. Lu Lu H. Holmes (1946 July–1948 April in Japan), who was a graduate of Teachers College, Columbia University and Dean of Women at Washington State College and Helen M. Hosp (1948 July–1950 April in Japan), who was a graduate of Goucher College and New York University and a former Dean of Women at the University of Nebraska (Roden, 1983), contributed very much to the new women's higher education in Japan.

Because Holmes had experience teaching history in Kobe Jogakuin as a visiting professor from 1934–35, she was familiar with women's higher education in Japan. Although there was no association between Holmes and Hosp who took over Holmes' duties, there were some common points between them. 1. Both of them were born around 1900 and had spent their college lives around 1920 when America reformed women's higher education. The number of women enjoying higher education gradually increased and some of them began to choose jobs instead of marriage. Both Holmes and Hosp were single women who had professional jobs. 2. They were Deans of Women in coeducational universities and helped female students adjust to the atmosphere of coeducation physically and psychologically. They also advised female students with their lives after finishing higher education. 3. They were members of the American Association of University Women (Tsuchiya, 1994).

The most prominent contribution of Ms. Holmes to women's higher education in Japan was helping women's *senmongakkô* become women's colleges. In 1948, 12 special schools including Nihon Joshi Daigakkô, Tokyo Joshi Daigaku, Tsuda Juku Senmongakkô, Seishin Joshi Gakuin and Kobe Jogakuin Senmongakkô were promoted to colleges, and in February, 1949, 79 special schools also became colleges. In the same year in May, 67 more special schools including Tokyo Joshi Koto Shihan Gakkô and Nara Joshi Koto Shihan Gakkô were promoted (Uemura, 1995). According to Ms. Holmes (1948), the reason why women's colleges were needed so urgently at that time were: 1. The colleges which had existed before were already full of male students coming back from World War II, 2. They were not prepared to handle female students such as providing dormitories for them, considering female students' health on campus and the relationships which should occur between male and female students on campus, 3. There was no suitable curriculum for female students, 4. Women's colleges were required because the level of secondary education between boys and girls was different before World War II and because female students needed time to get used to the new atmosphere of coeducation.

Ms. Holmes also contributed to setting up the standards for the colleges. Following American ideas about accreditation, an association was organized by representatives from existing colleges to give permission to a new institution when it was to be promoted as a college. She and other members in the mission held conferences where representatives from colleges in Japan decided the standards for establishing them. Their conferences were divided into three parts. One was deciding on the standards of coeducational universities focusing on literature. Another was doing the same for coeducational colleges emphasizing science. Still another was for women's colleges in general. For these women's colleges, five members were selected as a committee from Tokyo Joshi Koto Shihan Gakkô, Tsuda Juku Senmongakkô, Nihon Joshi

Daigakkô, Tokyo Joshi Daigaku and Seishin Joshi Gakuin. The reason for studying the role of the women's college in some depth was to discuss women's institutional problems which were different from those of coeducational institutions. The part concerning women's colleges was further divided into three parts for management of colleges, counseling and guidance, and minimum standards for curriculum. Ms. Holmes offered advice for all parts, and proposed introducing experts for counseling at women's colleges (Tsuchiya, 1994).

Holmes suggested and helped to establish the Japanese Association of College Alumnae (JACA). This association started their activities with the purpose of developing Japanese women's education in October 1946. The former organization of this association was a Japanese branch of the American Association of University Women (AAUW) set up in 1919. Though the Japanese branch of AAUW disappeared naturally during World War II, it was recovered as JACA by alumna from women's *senmongakkô* (Ito, 1990) and the Japanese branch of AAUW members who were Ms. Hoshino Aiko, President of Tsuda Juku Senmongakkô, Ms. Kamishiro Tano, later President of Nihon Joshi Daigakkô and Ms. Fujita Taki, the first president of JACA and later President of Tsuda Juku Senmongakkô (Uemura, 1995).

After it was established, JACA set up three committees: a committee for an educational system, a committee for deciding accreditation and a committee of JACA examiners. The committee for the educational system supported the 6-3-3-4 educational system absolutely which had been decided on by the first American mission and the Japanese committee following the war. The committee for deciding accreditation worked deciding on the standard of women's college education for the future and lifting the level of existing *senmongakkô*. The committee of JACA examiners helped *senmongakkô* so that they could be promoted to colleges by advising and arranging their curriculums (Itô, 1990).

The purposes of JACA were: 1. To arouse female ideas that women needed higher education in order to develop women's higher education in Japan and act as a pressure group against the Japanese government by following Donovan's statement that all associations in Japan should be used to arouse positive opinions about coeducation, equal opportunities of education and opening all types of occupations to women, and 2. To develop a female group which would carry out anything encouraging based on democracy and independence (Itô, 1990). Holmes found it necessary not only to reform education but also to awaken women to bringing up children, required by this new era. It was also necessary for women in Japan to learn about occupations they would be interested in and produce further demand for female workers by first understanding the meaning and importance of women's safety and mental independence, in performing well, as well as developing their ability to vote intelligently (Uemura, 1995).

Ms. Hosp, who took over Holmes' duties, introduced guidance (counseling services) to Japanese education. She said that guidance should be seriously considered as well as curriculum based on the idea that, because college was a place of learning for all people in a democratic society, college culture should echo this with mutual respect and trust among professors, personnel and students in fertile evidence (Uemura, 1995). She placed focus on helping female students in coeducational colleges solve their problems in new environments. Without such consideration, women's attendance in coeducational colleges might well have been curtailed. She offered meetings with female students to give advice on how to adjust to this new coeducational atmosphere and how to contribute to society after graduation. She asked the colleges to offer well-managed dormitories to female students and to hire female professors (Tsuchiya, 1994).

Ms. Hosp also suggested to the Japanese government to put in place a system of hiring deans of women and to have training courses to develop them. She insisted upon the necessity of having female professors as deans of women who had special training in guidance (Uemura, 1995). From October 10 to December 23, 1949 she held the first training course for deans of women and female faculty from colleges all over Japan under the auspice of the Ministry of Education. Seventeen women including three married women, three war widows and 11 unmarried women, were gathered. The format of the training course was relaxed and informal. There was no vertical relationship, which was often recognized in Japanese classrooms, between Hosp and the students. They had lectures on democracy, coeducation, student dormitories, women and occupations, new families and marriage and seminars to discuss them. They also had audio-visual aids such as movies, inspections of schools, libraries and government institutions, opportunities of having meetings with each other, and methods of counseling and orientations for new students (Rodon, 1983).

There were several main points arranged by Ms. Hosp, coordinator of this program, about this first training course. First, she had students decide topics of lectures, chairpersons for each date, and the plans of inspections and exercises. Second, she tried to help them understand their interests, talents and characters by using unforced counseling in order to obtain abilities which would be adjusted to new environments. Third, she emphasized that having a teaching position was valuable as opposed to simply getting married, insisting on the importance of including vocational elements in higher education. Since there were many unmarried teachers who felt the sting of inferiority due to a lingering Japanese ideology which insulted unmarried women, Ms. Hosp mentioned that having a job, without marriage, meant neither lack of womanly elements nor the need to feel inferior. She further explained the importance of women's economic independence, and an education which included vocational elements and methods of vocational education.

Hosp's training course aimed at lifting women's social position and training new women who were not only good wives and wise mothers at home but who also participated in social activities through their own skilled occupations. In her last class she asked each student to write her a letter including each student's small personal history in order to build up a friendship between she and her students. They not only told her their secrets to have her understand them but also tried to continue a strong open-ended relationship with her when they returned to their own countries (Uemura, 1995).

Although this training course was highly successful on the part of those who participated and there were a lot of requests to follow up on what had happened, this type of course was not continued after Ms. Hosp left Japan. However, the contributions she made, which remained after she left, were counseling services, guidance for finding jobs, and the careful orientations after students entered colleges (Tsuchiya, 1994).

The efforts of the American occupation, including the American mission and the two American female educators to reform Japan, continued until 1952. Without American aid, it was doubtful whether women's higher education in Japan would have developed as it has. Such aids contributed not only to the reform of education in Japan but also to making new Japanese laws which very much influenced improvement in women's higher education. The relationship between the new Japanese laws and women's education will be discussed in the next part.

2) New Laws and New Education Systems

In order to build a peaceful, democratic, new Japanese nation following the ideas of the Potsdam Declaration it was first necessary for Japan to establish a new constitution by abolishing the old one, Dai Nippon Teikoku Kenpô, which was set up in 1889 (Ienaga, 1977). In October, 1945, General Douglas MacArthur had in fact required the Japanese government to draw up a new constitution. The Government then set up a committee related to this issue and submitted ideas on the new constitution to MacArthur. However, after looking over the ideas drawn up by the Japanese committee, he recognized that it was difficult for Japan, which did not understand well what a real democracy was, to establish this new constitution. For this reason, he had Japan create the new constitution based on a concrete draft drawn up by the CIE. This is what was then called the MacAthur Draft (Nakajima, 1970). After making up the new constitution based on the draft, the Japanese government promulgated Nihonkoku Kenpô (the Japanese Constitution) on November 3, 1946 and made it fully operational by May 3, 1947.

The Nihonkoku Kenpô is composed of a preamble, 11 chapters and 103 articles. The basic principles listed in the preamble are democracy, respecting individual dignities (human rights) and pacifism. It also discusses the importance of harmony with foreign countries. Following this preamble, Chapter 1 points out that the Emperor, symbol of the Japanese people, no longer has absolute power to control everything. Chapter 2 describes that Japan will not have military service (only a self-defense force), which meant, in effect, abandonment of its power to wage wars. It describes the people's rights and duties including those to an education in Chapter 3, the National Diet in Chapter 4, the Cabinet in

Chapter 5, a court of justice in Chapter 6, finances in Chapter 7, local self-government in Chapter 8, articles for revising the constitution in Chapter 9, supreme regulations elevating the constitution to the highest level in law in Chapter 10 and certain supplementary rules in Chapter 11 (Mori, 1991b).

The point which should be asserted here is that the new Japanese constitution includes educational regulations which were not discussed in the old Japanese constitution. Before World War II, the Japanese Emperor controlled everything with absolute power. The old Japanese constitution was granted by the Emperor for the country (Nakajima, 1970). The Japanese government thus emphasized the national feeling that the Japanese nation was one big family organized by the Emperor, the ruling parent, who had absolute power over his citizen children, who always had to follow what the parent ordered. Basically, it was thought that because of the idea that parents should take responsibility for their children's education, educational affairs about the Japanese citizens were the Emperor's business. For this reason, before World War II there were no educational regulations in the old constitution, while rules associated with education were promulgated as ordinances from the master (the Emperor himself) to his subjects. A famous example was Educational Ordinance 'Kyôiku Chokugo'[10] promulgated in 1890, which included the Emperor's statements about educational rules for his citizens, emphasizing moral education based on Japanese Confucianism. This Ordinance was abolished with the old constitution after World War II. The new Japanese democratic constitution was created through decisions reached in committee by Japanese and American members having reached consensus about laws to be followed in practice by the Japanese public.

---

[10] It is the Imperial Rescript on Education.

There are some articles in Chapter 3 related to equal opportunities in education. Article 14, paragraph 1 describes that all citizens are equal under the law and should not be discriminated against politically, economically and socially because of race, creed, sex, social status or background. Article 23 in this chapter also mentions that all citizens are guaranteed freedom of education. In addition, article 26, paragraph 1 says that all citizens have the right to receive an education commensurate with their abilities to perform under the law, while paragraph 2 states that all citizens have a duty under the law to compel their children, both boys and girls, to go to school, free of charge. From these articles it is clear that the new Japanese constitution declared women's right to receive education to be the same rights as those for men. Furthermore, Chapter 3, article 24, paragraph 1 makes a point that marriage should be concluded only by two people's agreement and that married life should be kept based on equal rights and mutual cooperation (Mori, 1991b). Here, equal rights between the couples are made clear and women's social status and rights in Japan are seen as equal to that of men under the law.

Although some regulations relating to education were included in the new Japanese constitution, it was impossible to anticipate all of the important educational rules to be put into it. At that time Mr. Tanaka Kôtarô, the Minister of Education, explained the necessity of creating a law under which educational policies and systems could be discussed and proposed in meeting. Assembling for this purpose was held in June and July 1946 to correct the old Japanese constitution. Mr. Tanaka said that this law should be made up based on democracy and pacifism as mentioned in the new Japanese constitution, without including the Emperor's statements (Suzuki & Hirahara, 1998). Work for designing a new law on education was begun by a Japanese committee and a draft of the law was submitted to CIE on November 14, 1946 (Suzuki, 1983). This law, based on Japanese independence, was different from the law in the new Japanese constitution on education based on the draft made by CIE. After discussing the contents of this law between CIE and the Japanese committee, Kyôiku Kihonhô (The Fundamental Law of Education) was completed, promulgated and put into effect on March 31, 1947. The law was then amended and enforced on December 22, 2006 (The Ministry of Education, Culture, Sports, Science and Technology, 2006).

Kyôiku Kihonhô in 1947 was composed of a preamble and 11 articles. The first paragraph in the preamble emphasized the importance of education in building a democratic, civilized nation that would contribute to peace and human welfare in the world based on the new Japanese constitution. The second paragraph pointed out that the Japanese nation needed to offer education to help citizens build up their culture individually, respecting individual dignities and developing human beings who would demand truth and peace. It mainly focused on respecting individual human rights, reinforcing the meaning that no one needed to become a victim of either the nation or the Emperor.

Following this, the purpose of education was talked about in the first article, educational policies in the second, equal opportunities of education in the third,[11] compulsory education in the fourth, coeducation in the fifth,[12] school education in the sixth, social education in the seventh, political education in the eighth, religious in the ninth, educational administration in the 10th and finally, supplementary rules in the 11th. The equal opportunities for education in the

---

11 The equal opportunities for education are discussed in the fourth article in the revised Fundamental Law of Education.

12 The coeducation in the fifth article has been eliminated because it is very common today.

third article prohibited educational segregation by declaring no differences in educational opportunities between men and women. It meant that both men and women had equal rights to receiving education, opening higher education to all women. What's more, the coeducation in the fifth article said that because men and women should respect and cooperate with each other, coeducation should be permitted (Naitô, 1998). It operated on the assumption that women should be treated the same as men are in the halls of education.

At the same time that Kyôiku Kihonhô was promulgated, the Gakkô Kyôikuhô (the School Education Act) was created as well. While Kyôiku Kihonhô discusses educational ideas and principles, Gakkô Kyôikuhô lays out the school systems (Suzuki, 1999). Gakkô Kyôikuhô was promulgated on March 31 and enforced on April 1, 1947. It was established to achieve the purpose discussed in the 26th article of the Nihonkoku Kenpô as well as the Kyôiku Kihonhô. Some parts of the Gakkô Kyôikuhô were revised sometime after 1947.

There are six characteristics to Gakkô Kyôikuhô: 1. A single track educational idea asserting a 6–3–3–4 system to help students win more opportunities to advance onto further education by abolishing the old plural track educational system. 2, The period of compulsory education became longer (from six to nine years) by establishing the middle school whose period is three years. 3. In order to expand educational opportunities for working students, part-time high schools and colleges are established as well as correspondence courses and open lectures in colleges. This law sets up the procedure for disability students to finish compulsory education. 4. The idea of abolishing educational discrepancies between boys and girls replaced the different levels of content curriculum that had existed between the two. 5. Private schools were allowed to keep their own educational independence instead of adhering to the overall system of supervision by the Japanese government. 6. Content of curriculum includes a lot of democratic and flexible elements, thus avoiding strict content uniformity (Mori, 1991b).

The Gakkô Kyôikuhô in 1947 was composed of nine chapters and 110 articles.[13] It described the common elements about all schools in Chapter 1, elementary schools in Chapter 2, middle schools in Chapter 3, high schools in Chapter 4, universities in Chapter 5, schools for disability students in Chapter 6, kindergartens in Chapter 7, others in Chapter 8 and punishments in Chapter 9. The universities in Chapter 5[14] included 19 articles related to junior college, college and graduate school, presenting their purposes, courses, correspondence education, the periods required to finish a program, qualifications to enter, faculty and degrees (Kobayashi, 1951).

The new college system installed in Japan after World War II was an advanced higher education system including elements of American education which took the place of the old Japanese colleges, *senmongakkô* and *shihangakkô*. One national college was established in each prefecture and the number of colleges increased (Nara Joshi Daigaku 60 nenshi Henshû Iinkai, 1970). The purpose of the new higher education system in Japan was to educate leaders to support Japan as a peaceful and civilized nation. Its main function was to pursue academic education, respect the liberal arts, while helping students become all-round citizens of Japanese society, and additionally emphasizing technical and special education through vocational training. Following these ideas, in 1947 Gakkô Kyôikuhô prescribed that the college, as the center of learning, must offer a variety of knowledge including

---

13 The Gakkô Kyôikuhô is composed of 13 chapters and 146 articles now.
14 Now, universities are discussed in Chapter 9 with 32 articles.

thorough exposure to special arts and sciences in depth in order to develop intellectual, ethical and applied capacities. Gakkô Kyôikuhô is the regulation that states not just the purpose of the college, but also its character, which is different from that of the old Japanese imperial universities and colleges. This regulation is also based on democracy and liberalism without over-emphasizing nationalism (Murata, 1980).

Gakkô Kyôikuhô in 1947 prescribed that the junior college offered a two or three year education program to the student who finished high school. It was a well-rounded educational system which focused on special education for vocation while considering liberal arts, and it aimed at fullness of adult education and popularization of college education (Murata, 1980). The junior college arrangement very much contributed to women's higher education in Japan after World War II. Basically this system was established to save *senmongakkô* which could not promote themselves as four-year colleges because of inappropriate facilities and other reasons.

The American mission also mentioned the need for a graduate school level of attainment with all of its functions. In order to pursue truth fully, a system of graduate schools was required, it being necessary for such a school to stimulate and support both professors and advanced students in a variety of ways. The purpose of the graduate school is to train excellent students with deep knowledge and capacity to pursue their special fields and find those educators who would lead these students, thus contributing to making the academic level higher in all areas of thought by creative studies. The graduate school is not only an educational institution but also the institution which leads in research and study. Better facilities for doing research and a system of scholarship for high achieving students needed to be provided immediately (Murata, 1980).

In 1950, private graduate schools and in 1953, public graduate schools were established in order to accept the first graduates into the new system. At first, only new colleges stemming from old Japanese schools were allowed to set up graduate schools as institutes independent of their colleges. These graduate schools also accepted female students just as four-year and junior colleges did. Many curriculums were decided on to fit the new purposes in the new graduate schools. After finishing such programs, students were allowed to receive their advanced degrees. New colleges established after World War II were also permitted to set up graduate institutions which were expected to develop their own professional fields in similar ways (Murata, 1980).

Influenced by these educational reforms, some female colleges which were promoted in 1948, also changed their educational system. Nihon Joshi Daigaku (old name, Nihon Joshi Daigakkô) began accepting new school systems based on new educational laws established in 1947 as it reopened its kindergarten, changed its elementary school's name *kôtô jogakkô* into a middle school, and set up its high school before starting its new women's college. This is a school which from the beginning at kindergarten has a connected line of development into a college education. In 1948, it started with two departments; home economics and literature. The department of home economics was composed of six courses; namely, child study, food, life arts, social welfare, physics-and-chemistry, and biology-and-agriculture. Its department of literature held Japanese literature, English literature and history, adding education in 1950. In 1952, this school established its own research center for home economics, setting up a graduate school for child study and food courses in 1961. This was the earliest establishment of a graduate school for home economics in private colleges in Japan. In 1952, this school also set up academies for each of the courses (Aoki,

1981).

In 1948, Tsuda Juku Daigaku was also promoted to a small college, having no separate department per se and only an English course. In July, 1948, the President, Ms. Hoshino, described, "The new policy in this new school is to emphasize liberal arts, aiming at higher general education in addition to special vocational programs in order to train students who would be open-minded, flexible and able to accept new ideas well. For this reason, students at this school need to finish some common liberal arts in addition to their English education." Tsuda Juku Daigaku required students to choose more than two subjects from those related to the humanities, social sciences, and natural science. The school prohibited students from taking only those subjects associated with English because of their focus of interest while it offered students many subjects so that they could enjoy an enhancement of choices (Ishii, 2000). In 1949, this school had a mathematics course, adding a graduate school program for mathematics in 1965. In 1963, it established a graduate school for the English course. In addition, in 1974 it set up a graduate school for international affairs (Tsuda Juku Daigaku 90 shûnen Kinen Jigyô Shuppan Iinkai, 1990).

In addition to Nihon Joshi Daigaku and Tsuda Juku Daigaku, Tokyo Joshi Daigaku, established by six Christian organizations, was promoted to a college in the same year with a literature department composed of philosophy, Japanese literature and English and American literature courses. In 1950, it added a social science course. That same year it set up academies for each course to give its faculty a place to present their research. Because of public demand, in 1966 this school re-established its junior college with an English and education course. The English course focused on offering practical English by understanding international affairs. It did so with both lectures and seminars emphasizing small class size. The education course aimed at training students who would have wide knowledge and rich receptivity, including social science, physiology, literature and natural science. In 1979, this course offered gender education as a required subject in order to understand and improve on the women's situation in society. In 1988, its four-year college added a current culture department composed of communication, local culture and language culture courses. This department aimed at training students who would contribute to society with an international sensibility and an ability to manage information. In 1971, a graduate school was set up for Japanese literature, English and American literature and mathematics courses and in 1976, a philosophy course (Tokyo Joshi Daigaku 80 nenshi Henshû Iinkai, 1998).

Nara Joshi Daigaku (Nara Women's University) was promoted to a college in 1949. Since it began as a national college, it had to follow the Ministry of Education's decision establishing the college under the new system started in 1949, while some private colleges had already begun a new system in 1948 using the CIE guidelines. Nara Joshi Daigaku is not a normal school any longer but a general college. Students needing a teaching certificate could obtain one after finishing some additional subjects. This was the biggest change after World War II for this school. Furthermore, because the policies of this school were always very much associated with national policies emphasizing women's morals and the idea of a good wife and wise mother, this new school now reflected, in a way, how to obtain freedom and emancipation from old customs. Individual students were respected equally as human beings despite gender differences, and they had access to free communication with one another by abolishing the requirement of living in a dormitory with many strict rules. It had two departments, literature and science-home economics. The literature department was composed of five courses in the areas of sociology, Japanese literature, English literature, history and geology. The science-home economics area also had five courses: mathematics, physics-and-chemistry, biology, childcare-and-health and clothing. In 1952, an education course including physical education was added to the literature department, and the following year home economics became independent from the science-home economics department. Finally, a graduate school for home economics was established in 1964, and one for science the next year (Nara Joshi Daigaku 60 nenshi Henshû Iinkai, 1970).

3) Post War Number of Schools, Female Students and the Courses They Selected

After coeducation in national colleges began in 1946, private colleges were also opened to female students. Tables 9 and 10 describe the number of colleges (universities) and junior colleges based on separate and coed schools respectively. Almost 70% of all the colleges mentioned here had graduate schools (Mabashi, 1995). In 1955, there were 13 male colleges (universities) while only four male schools were left in 2010. The number of female colleges (universities) increased more than three times between 1955 and 2000, although it decreased in 2010. The total number of colleges (universities) also increased from 228 to 778 between 1955 and 2010, female colleges (universities) numbering 10 or 11% of all col-

Table 9: The number of colleges (universities) with college students based on separate and coed schools

	male only	female only	coed	total
1955	13	32	189	228
1960	12	37	196	245
1965	3	62	242	317(131)
1970	3	81	298	382(180)
1975	1	83	334	420(213)
1980	2	88	354	446(257)
1985	0	80	377	460(281)
1990	1	90	414	507(313)
1995	0	94	467	565(385)
2000	1	97	544	649(544)
2005	0	86	627	726(569)
2010	4	81	666	778(616)

( ) represents the number of graduate schools
Total includes the number of schools without students.

Table 10: The number of junior colleges with students based on separate and coed schools

	male only	female only	coed	total
1955	27	118	119	264
1960	23	140	117	280
1965	18	216	130	364
1970	9	302	165	476
1975	10	310	191	511
1980	4	312	197	513
1985	4	322	210	543
1990	1	339	246	593
1995	2	322	268	596
2000	3	252	306	572
2005	2	166	299	488
2010	0	122	263	395

Total includes the number of schools without students.

Table 11: The number of colleges (universities) based on national, public and private schools

	national	public	private	total
1955	72(2)	34(4)	122(26)	228(32)
1960	72(2)	33(5)	140(103)	245(37)
1965	73(2)	35(6)	209(54)	317(62)
1970	75(2) [59]	33(6) [19]	274(73) [102]	382(81)
1975	81(2) [66]	34(7) [18]	305(74) [129]	420(83)
1980	93(2) [77]	34(8) [21]	319(78) [159]	446(88)
1985	95(2) [88]	34(8) [22]	331(70) [171]	460(80)
1990	96(2) [95]	39(7) [23]	372(81) [195]	507(90)
1995	98(2) [98]	52(6) [31]	415(86) [256]	565(94)
2000	99(2) [99]	72(5) [50]	478(90) [330]	649(97)
2005	87(2) [87]	86(5) [74]	580(79) [408]	753(86)
2010	86(2) [86]	95(7) [80]	597(72) [450]	778(81)

( ) represents the number of female schools within the total number
[ ] shows the number of graduate schools

Table 12: The number of junior colleges based on national, public and private schools

	national	public	private	total
1955	17(0)	43(13)	204(105)	264(118)
1960	27(0)	39(15)	214(125)	280(140)
1965	28(0)	39(17)	297(199)	364(216)
1970	22(0)	43(17)	411(285)	476(302)
1975	31(1)	48(23)	432(286)	511(310)
1980	35(1)	50(23)	428(288)	513(312)
1985	37(0)	51(21)	455(301)	543(322)
1990	41(1)	54(21)	498(317)	593(339)
1995	36(0)	60(18)	500(304)	596(322)
2000	20(0)	55(9)	497(243)	572(252)
2005	10(3)	42(6)	436(157)	488(166)
2010	0	26(4)	369(118)	395(122)

( ) represents the number of female schools within the total number
Sources: *Gakkô Kihon Chôsa Hôkokusho*, 1956, 1961, 1966, 1971, 1976, 1981, 1986, 1991, 1996, 2001, 2006 and 2011.

leges (universities). Regarding junior colleges, in 1955 there were 27 male junior colleges while in 2010 they were closed. After 1964 when the system of junior colleges became permanent, the number of these schools increased sharply. Especially between 1965 and 1975, more than 100 junior colleges were established, the total number of them incresing from 264 to 596 between 1955 and 1995. The number of junior colleges decreased after 1995 because some of them disappeared due to the Japanese economic downturn and the lack of enough eligible 18-year-old people to fill them. Female junior colleges were 45% of all junior colleges in 1955, 54% in 1995 and 30% in 2010 (The Ministry of Education in Japan, 1956, 1961, 1966, 1971, 1976, 1981, 1986, 1991, 1996 a and 2001; The Ministry of Education, Culture, Sports, Science and Technology in Japan, 2006 and 2011).

Tables 11 and 12 focus on the number of colleges (universities) and junior colleges based on being national, public or private. The numbers in the parentheses tell us the number of female schools within the total number. There were only two national female universities: Ochanomizu Joshi Daigaku (old name, Tokyo Joshi Kôtô Shihan Gakkô) and Nara Joshi Daigaku (old name, Nara Joshi Kôtô Shihan Gakkô). The number of public female colleges (universities) was seven in 2011 and 93% of all female colleges (universities) were private schools. The number of national and public female schools changed little between 1955 and 2000 while private female schools increased from 26 to 90, more than three times as many. However, they decreased after 2000. As for junior colleges, since 1955 there has been no national female junior college, though there were some exceptions. There were four public ones which was 3.3% of all female junior colleges while there were 118 private women's junior colleges, which was 97% of them in 2010. As these tables show, Japanese education was supported by private institutions very much in terms of both coed and female-only education (The Ministry of Education in Japan, 1956, 1961, 1966, 1971, 1976, 1981, 1986, 1991, 1996 a and 2001; The Ministry of Education, Culture, Sports, Science and Technology in Japan, 2006 and 2011).

Tables 13, 14 and 15 represent the number of students in colleges (universities), graduate schools and junior colleges. Table 13 mentions the number of students in both undergraduate and graduate schools together while Table 14 refers only to the number of students in graduate schools. The number of female students within the total is in parentheses. The percentage of female students increased year by year. For example, in 1955, 12.4% of all students were female but in 2010 female students were 41.1% of the total number of students in colleges (universities). In focusing on female students in graduate schools, their percentage also increased

Table 13 : The number of students in colleges (universities)

	total	national	public	private	% of women	% of private
1955	523,355(65,081)	186,055	24,936	312,364	12.4	59.7
1960	626,421(85,966)	194,227	28,569	403,625	13.7	64.4
1965	937,556(152,119)	238,380	38,277	660,899	16.2	70.5
1970	1,406,521(252,745)	309,587	50,111	1,046,823	18.0	74.4
1975	1,734,082(368,258)	357,772	50,880	1,325,430	21.2	76.4
1980	1,835,312(405,529)	406,644	52,082	1,376,586	22.1	75.0
1985	1,848,698(434,401)	449,373	54,944	1,344,381	23.5	72.7
1990	2,133,362(584,155)	518,609	64,140	1,550,613	27.4	72.7
1995	2,546,649(821,893)	598,723	83,812	1,864,114	32.3	73.2
2000	2,740,023(992,312)	624,082	107,198	2,008,743	36.2	73.3
2005	2,865,051(1,124,900)	627,850	124,910	2,112,291	39.3	73.7
2010	2,887,414(1,185,580)	625,048	142,523	2,119,843	41.1	73.4

Table 14 : The number of students in graduate schools

	Total	national	public	private	% of women	% of private
1955	10,174(593)	5,022	409	4,743	5.8	46.6
1960	15,734(1,113)	8,928	851	5,955	7.1	37.8
1965	28,454(2,143)	16,809	2,146	9,499	7.5	33.4
1970	40,957(3,576)	23,547	2,301	15,109	8.7	36.9
1975	48,464(4,547)	27,735	2,323	18,406	9.4	38.0
1980	53,992(6,259)	32,728	2,386	18,878	11.6	35.0
1985	69,688(9,182)	43,049	3,006	23,633	13.2	33.9
1990	90,238(14,566)	57,885	3,890	28,463	16.1	31.5
1995	153,423(32,990)	97,704	6,555	49,164	21.5	32.0
2000	205,311(54,216)	128,624	9,719	66,968	26.4	32.6
2005	254,480(75,734)	150,780	13,928	89,772	29.8	35.3
2010	271,454(82,133)	157,092	16,403	97,959	30.3	36.1

from 5.8% to 30.3%, almost five times. The difference between colleges (universities) and graduate schools was that most of the students in colleges (universities) belonged to private institutions while many graduate students attended

Table 15 : The number of students in junior colleges

	Total	national	public	private	% of women	% of private
1955	77,885(42,061)	3,637	11,080	63,168	54.0	81.1
1960	83,457(56,357)	6,652	11,086	65,719	67.5	78.7
1965	147,563(110,388)	8,060	13,603	125,900	74.8	85.3
1970	263,219(217,668)	9,886	16,136	237,197	82.7	90.1
1975	353,782(305,124)	13,143	17,973	322,666	86.2	91.2
1980	371,124(330,468)	14,685	19,002	337,437	89.0	90.0
1985	371,095(333,175)	17,530	20,767	332,798	89.8	89.7
1990	479,389(438,443)	18,510	22,647	438,232	91.5	91.4
1995	498,516(455,439)	13,735	24,134	460,647	91.4	92.4
2000	327,680(293,690)	7,772	21,061	298,847	89.6	91.2
2005	219,355(191,131)	1,643	14,347	203,365	87.1	92.7
2010	155,273(137,791)	0	9,128	146,145	88.7	94.1

( ) represents the number of female students within the total figures
Surce: *Monbu Tôkei Yôran*, 2001 and *Monbu Kagaku Tôkei Yôran*, 2011.

national or public institutions. For instance, in 2010, 73.4% of all college (university) students studied in private schools while only 36.1% of those in graduate schools continued their work in private schools (The Ministry of Education, Culture, Sports and Technology in Japan, 2011). This meant that national and public schools in Japan had better facilities and atmosphere than private schools to build their achievements upon. Because Japanese education is still strongly controlled by high government standards, people tend to think national and public schools offer better education than private schools although there are many good private schools. Entrance examinations for national and public schools are generally more difficult than those of private schools and they are more famous. The Japanese people's way of thinking is that smart people have privileges and can receive better education without spending a lot of money simply because they are smart. For this reason, the good students tend to 'find a home' for their abilities at national and public schools.

An amazing thing about junior colleges was that almost 90% of the students were women and in addition, more than 90% of these students belonged to private institutions after 1975 (The Ministry of Education in Japan, 2001; The Ministry of Education, Culture, Sports and Technology in Japan, 2011). We can say that women's private junior colleges very much contributed to women's higher education in Japan. Most of the students in national junior colleges were men; there were very few female students there. There were some, but not many, female students who were studying in public junior colleges. We can not see any national junior colleges in 2010. They were closed because of lack of money.

Tables 16 and 17 talk about the percentage of students going to college or junior college, after students finish their high school level of education. In 1955, the percentage of female students going to a four-year college was 2.4% of all the female students finishing high school and that of those going to junior college was 2.6%. The total percentage of women attending higher education was 5.0% of that total while that of male students was 15%, which was 13.1% (college) and 1.9% (junior college). Total percentage of male students going on to higher education was almost three and a half times that of female students. Ten years later, in 1965, the total percentage of female students going to higher education was 11.3% (college, 4.6% and junior college, 6.7%) while that of male students was 22.4% (college, 20.7% and junior college, 1.7%). Male students' percentages were still almost twice that of female students. In 1990, however, women's percentages became larger than those of men. Table 16 recorded female, 37.4% (college, 15.2% and junior college, 22.2%) and male 35.1% (college, 33.4% and junior college, 1.7%). The thing to focus on is that the percentage of female students going to junior college increased tremendously. It

Table 16 : The percentage of students going to college

	male	female	total
1955	13.1	2.4	7.9
1960	13.7	2.5	8.2
1965	20.7	4.6	12.8
1970	27.3	6.5	17.1
1975	41.0	12.7	27.2
1980	39.3	12.3	26.1
1985	38.6	13.7	26.5
1990	33.4	15.2	24.6
1995	40.7	22.9	32.1
2000	47.5	31.5	39.7
2005	51.3	36.8	44.2
2010	56.4	45.2	50.9

Table 17 : The percentage of students going to junior college

	male	female	total
1955	1.9	2.6	2.2
1960	1.2	3.0	2.1
1965	1.7	6.7	4.1
1970	2.0	11.2	6.5
1975	2.6	20.2	11.2
1980	2.0	21.0	11.3
1985	2.0	20.8	11.1
1990	1.7	22.2	11.7
1995	2.1	24.6	13.1
2000	1.9	17.2	9.4
2005	1.8	13.0	7.3
2010	1.3	10.8	5.9

was only 2.6% in 1955 while in 1990 it changed to 22.2% which was 10 times as much. On the other hand, the percentage of male students going to junior college remained about 2%, not much change here (The Ministry of Education in Ja-

Table 18 : The percentage of students going to graduate school

	male	female	total
1965	4.7	1.9	4.2
1970	5.1	1.5	4.4
1975	5.1	1.7	4.3
1980	4.7	1.6	3.9
1985	6.5	2.5	5.5
1990	7.7	3.1	6.4
1995	10.7	5.5	9.0
2000	12.8	6.3	10.3
2005	14.8	7.2	11.6
2010	17.4	7.1	12.9

Sources: *Monbu Tôkei Yôran,* 2001 and *Monbu Kagaku Tôkei Yôran,* 2011.

pan, 2001). Until 1995, the percentage of female students going to junior college was higher than those going to college but it changed in 1995 because most big companies tended to hire college graduate female students rather than junior college graduate female students after the Japanese economic downturn. They needed capable female power in order to contribute to the recovery of the Japanese economic situation.

Table 18 discusses the percentage of those going to graduate school. In 1965, only 1.9% of all female students finishing college went on to graduate school while 4.7% of all male students obtaining college degrees did so. The percentage of female students going to graduate school increased and by 2010 it rose to 7.1%. Yet, this was still less than half of the percentage of male students, 17.4% (The Ministry of Education, Culture, Sports, Science, and Technology in Japan, 2011).

Table 19, Table 20 and Table 21 represent the number of colleges, junior colleges and graduate students based on their majors. The most popular subject among college women in Table 19 was the humanities and the next one was education, the third being home economics in 1958. The percentage of female students studying humanities was 36% of all female students and that of those doing education was 26%. The number of students majoring in home economics and health was almost the same, their numbers being 8,500 and 8,458, respectively. In 1975, the number of female students learning humanities rose to more than that of male students and humanities was still the most popular discipline among women college students. Education also kept the second position but social science took the third instead of home economics. In 1990, social science took second place, its number being 114,930 or 21% of all. This percentage increased to 29%, 267,789 students in 2000, and it was quite close to the percentage of humanities (30%) whose number was 275,733. In 2005, social science took the first position and its number was 294,688. The most unpopular subject among female college students was the merchant marines. From 1958 to 1975, this number was included with 'others' until 1985 when this category became independent. Science, engineering and agriculture were also not so popular among women, although the number of college female students studying engineering and agriculture increased. Engineering began in 1958 with 254 female students, the percentage being 0.4% of all female students. In 2010, engineering was followed by 43,583 women students with the percentage of the whole rising to 4%. We can see the same situation happening with agriculture. Although the number of female students majoring in science increased, the percentage of those studying it was about 2%–4% of all the female students (The Ministry of Education in Japan, 1959 1966, 1976, 1986, 1991, 1996 b, and 2001; The Ministry of Education, Culture, Sports, Science and Technology in Japan 2006 and 2011). These fields were clearly static for male students.

When it came to popular subjects among junior college

female students, home economics won first place until 2000. The numbers of female students majoring in home economics was 25,120 in 1958 and 48,093 in 1965 and their percentages were 58% and 54% of all female students, respectively. In 1975, the number of female students studying home economics rose to 97,150 whose percentage was 32% of the whole but tended to decrease after 2000. Although in 1995, humanities took first position over home economics, home economics took it back in 2000. In 2005, education took the first position. Generally speaking, popular courses were education, home economics and humanities. Like the tendency among college female students, the social sciences also became popular among junior college female students while science, engineering and agriculture were not so popular (The Ministry of Education in Japan, 1959, 1966, 1976, 1986, 1991, 1996 b, and 2001; The Ministry of Education, Culture, Sports, Science and Technology in Japan 2006 and 2011). Like the tendency in four-year colleges, science, engineering and agriculture were still fields for male students. The number of students studying the arts was included with 'others' between 1958 and 1965 because its number was not large. General culture, begun before 1985, was a new subject. Students in this course learned about international cultures, obtaining knowledge helpful to international understandings.

Regarding female graduate students, in 1965 the most popular subject was the humanities, the second popular one science and the third being health. Generally, merchant marine was not popular among them. The interesting thing was the number of female students studying home economics was small, and this tendency was very different from that among four-year college and junior college female students (The Ministry of Education in Japan, 1959, 1966, 1976, 1986, 1991, 1996 b and 2001). Probably most of the people thought that home economics was not considered an academic subject which should be taken seriously in graduate school but a subject which should be learned more appropriately by future housewives. In 2010, health was the most popular, with humanities being second and others third (The Ministry of Education, Culture, Sports, Science and Technology in Japan, 2011).

Table 19 : The number of college students based on their majors

year	sex	humanities	social science	science	engineering	agriculture	health medicine	others	mercantile marine	arts	home economics	education	others	total
1958	m	66,441	213,586	14,121	72,137	26,356	26,661	0	0	0	140	40,567	10,443	470,452
	f	24,757	2,695	1,655	254	271	8,458	0	0	0	8,500	17,605	3,876	68,071
1965	m	68,511	330,600	20,939	154,426	33,885	21,921	0	0	0	23	29,185	29,214	688,704
	f	57,129	6,274	2,924	670	970	11,407	0	0	0	12,081	26,487	11,105	129,047
1975	m	86,988	635,224	42,981	331,060	53,163	43,486	0	18,140	0	703	49,265	34,826	1,295,836
	f	128,945	53,443	7,244	2,899	5,149	27,066	0	22,615	0	29,062	69,746	9,998	356,167
1985	m	100,117	608,561	48,890	334,215	51,240	61,724	16,706	1,486	16,195	247	65,217	15,410	1,320,008
	f	146,733	62,440	10,788	9,375	8,828	13,026	26,353	62	28,695	31,938	70,010	6,136	414,384
1990	m	103,096	672,395	54,451	375,461	52,806	54,101	17,820	1,463	16,440	528	64,516	20,829	1,433,906
	f	199,498	114,930	12,327	15,185	13,971	15,782	28,698	71	31,532	35,894	76,444	10,334	554,666
1995	m	123,907	733,987	63,254	421,379	46,528	46,738	17,769	875	19,868	1,186	62,725	24,729	1,562,945
	f	251,057	199,637	19,510	35,328	25,352	18,929	38,645	60	39,739	39,617	84,528	15,484	767,886
2000	m	135,246	717,828	65,619	420,673	41,981	42,965	22,982	803	20,114	2,160	56,455	31,707	1,558,533
	f	275,733	267,789	22,282	46,489	28,327	21,344	56,346	102	45,094	42,138	81,160	26,418	913,222
2005	m	133,586	651,068	64,683	387,674	41,878	42,018	39,056	403	22,293	4,921	55,511	55,780	1,498,871
	f	271,827	294,688	22,161	45,703	28,450	21,535	84,245	36	50,329	55,249	86,380	48,614	1,009,217
2010	m	130,099	604,082	60,417	357,050	44,822	43,480	64,103	4	21,028	6,815	68,070	81,439	1,481,409
	f	258,465	288,463	21,008	43,583	30,994	21,455	124,145	0	51,769	61,345	98,910	77,645	1,077,782

Table 20 : The number of junior college students based on their majors

	sex	humanities	social science	science & engineering	agriculture	health	general culture	home economics	education	arts	others	total
1958	m	4,531	14,131	7,234	1,160	0	0	24	299	0	759	28,138
	f	10,274	1,336	244	169	0	0	25,120	3,344	0	2,969	43,447
1965	m	2,448	17,925	13,884	1,425	0	0	69	77	0	454	36,282
	f	22,899	3,970	479	297	446	0	48,093	7,693	0	5,407	89,284
1975	m	1,586	17,190	22,455	3,541	913	0	219	287	1,346	83	47,620
	f	72,059	20,725	1,047	632	9,110	0	97,150	77,720	16,521	6,338	301,302
1985	m	1,687	10,896	16,759	3,165	2,558	165	158	540	1,256	24	37,208
	f	83,369	25,094	3,028	941	17,986	8,150	95,459	75,639	16,751	2,555	328,972
1990	m	1,996	12,297	17,519	2,455	3,232	51	277	555	1,741	26	40,149
	f	120,192	47,699	6,210	1,310	23,519	14,014	116,374	78,065	19,753	5,909	433,045
1995	m	3,233	13,464	16,374	1,951	2,766	16,296	886	838	2,150	33	57,991
	f	125,943	51,899	5,986	1,741	27,885	17,029	114,591	73,543	20,609	8,206	447,432
2000	m	3,135	8,865	10,098	1,468	3,241	190	1,296	1,945	1,958	367	32,563
	f	60,259	34,342	3,115	1,483	26,468	7,970	75,922	58,282	13,756	4,098	285,695
2005	m	2,339	5,787	7,606	1,204	2,337	68	1,676	3,889	1,105	1,044	27,055
	f	25,467	20,369	2,184	894	15,350	2,866	43,045	58,817	7,751	8,402	185,145
2010	m	1,473	3,584	3,547	815	1,592	17	1,191	2,461	671	1,072	16,423
	f	16,181	14,250	872	604	10,870	2,144	28,865	43,014	5,450	10,960	133,210

Table 21 : The number of graduate students based on their majors

	sex	humanities	social science	science	engineering	agriculture	health	home economics	mercantile marine	arts	education	others	total
1965	m	4,145	3,375	2,652	5,089	1,068	5,771	3	0	0	0	259	22,302
	f	868	160	272	39	59	243	95	0	0	0	107	1,843
1975	m	6,489	6,305	5,205	15,934	3,511	4,455	45	691	0	1,282	0	43,917
	f	1,951	489	376	102	188	358	260	370	0	453	0	4,547
1985	m	6,105	5,705	6,494	22,634	5,159	10,002	29	50	744	3,170	414	60,506
	f	2,767	1,105	576	437	830	1,113	347	0	632	1,295	80	9,182
1995	m	7,169	11,931	13,699	53,967	7,913	15,151	82	62	1,098	5,609	3,752	120,433
	f	7,213	4,957	2,487	3,319	2,061	4,401	863	5	1,336	4,669	1,679	32,990
2000	m	8,945	18,954	15,571	64,655	8,434	18,230	165	41	1,353	6,384	8,363	151,095
	f	10,160	8,698	3,624	6,239	3,580	8,313	992	5	1,930	5,995	4,680	54,216
2005	m	9,511	18,197	16,261	71,110	8,516	21,720	216	48	1,960	6,582	13,803	167,924
	f	11,603	9,942	4,248	8,405	4,173	13,504	1,231	9	2,958	6,833	8,627	71,533
2010	m	8,521	16,206	15,405	76,345	9,013	22,531	244	50	1,931	6,403	16,020	172,669
	f	11,362	10,096	3,970	9,583	4,521	15,023	1,173	20	3,258	6,442	10,144	75,592

The data doesn't include the number of students in professional degree programs.
Sources: *Monbu Tōkei Yōran*, 1959, 1966, 1976, 1986, 1991, 1996 b, 2001 and *Monbu Kagaku Tōkei Yōran*, 2006, 2011.

4) Post War Situation of Female Students and Their Institutions of Higher Education

The situation for female students in schools of higher education changed drastically after World War II. Coeducation in national colleges began in 1946 when 20 students entered Tokyo Daigaku[15] (old name, Tokyo Teikoku Daigaku) with a strong desire for learning (Amano, 1986). These students also had strong intentions of living as contributing human beings in society, making efforts to improve themselves after being emancipated from domestic work and subordination to men. For a time after the War the women felt tension in their college environment simply because of being women among men. Sometimes they needed to deny their sex in order to keep harmony with the male students. This situation gradually changed around 1955. After that time, high economic growth started in Japan and the growth of the Japanese economy developed 150 times from 1900 to 1970 (Ienaga, 1977). Following Japanese high economic growth, the number of female students going into higher education, especially junior colleges and four-year colleges, increased tremendously. For example, the number of female students finishing higher education multiplied more than 100 times from 1915 to 1970 while that of men increased only 14 times over. Moreover, the number of female students in higher education in 1950 was 200 times more than it was in 1915 and 600 times over by 1970 (Fujii, 1973). After 1960, female students in coed colleges felt less strange because of being women and became more familiar with college life as a whole. At the same time the meaning of higher education for women was altered from that of privilege for a small number of women to a

---

[15] Tokyo University

right for almost every woman, and finally a kind of social duty for women in the middle and upper classes. The purpose of the female students who went into higher education was also changed from obtaining professional techniques related to occupations in order to make a living, to emphasizing general knowledge through the liberal arts. College for female students was a place to enjoy their youth living with friends instead of a place where they pursued professional education under pressure (Amano, 1986).

Table 22 explained why female students in those days decided to go into higher institutions. This table presents opinions of female students from three female colleges and three female junior colleges in 1959. 37% of all the students (38% of the junior college students and 36.4% of the college students) said that they wanted to acquire general knowledge, while 23.7% of them (22% of the junior college students and 24.9% of the college students) said that they wanted to achieve a professional education (Minami, 1959).

Table 23 also described the purpose of having higher education of female students from Kobe Jogakuin Daigaku, a women's college and Kwansei Gakuin Daigaku, a coed college, from 1961 to 1965 and 1966 to 1970. From 1961 to 1965, the largest percentage was to obtain broad general knowledge (ratios being 85.9% at Kobe Jogakuin Daigaku and 83.7% at Kwansei Gakuin Daigaku), and the second largest percentage was to build up friendships (ratios being 45.7% and 53.5% respectively). On the other hand, the percentages of having a professional education were 42.4% at Kobe Jogakuin Daigaku and 39.5% at Kwansei Gakuin Daigaku, which were the third largest number in both colleges. (The total of these percentages was not 100% because students were allowed to choose plural answers.) The situation from 1966 to 1970 was almost as same as that from 1961 to 1965. Though considering only specific colleges to have a problem,

Table 22 : Why did you decide to go to your higher institution?

to get professional education	23.7%	junior college	22.0%
		college	24.9%
to get general knowledge	37.0%	junior college	38.0%
		college	36.4%
because of the school's fame	21.2%	junior college	28.6%
		college	16.8%
to obtain a good occupation	6.8%	junior college	1.9%
		college	9.8%
others	11.3%	junior college	9.5%
		college	12.1%
total	100%	total of J. C	100%
		total of C.	100%

Source: *Fujin Kôron*, 1959.

Table 23 : Purpose of having higher education

		1961 to 1965	1966 to 1970
Kobe Jogakuin	professional education	42.4%	39.6%
	general knowledge	85.9%	80.2%
	friendships	45.7%	45.3%
	to obtain qualifications	8.7%	15.1%
	to find a good job	4.3%	3.8%
	to find a good husband	1.1%	3.8%
Kwansei Gakuin	professional education	39.5%	30.7%
	general knowledge	83.7%	85.7%
	friendships	53.5%	52.1%
	to obtain qualifications	14.0%	11.4%
	to find a good job	2.3%	8.6%
	to find a good husband	2.3%	1.4%
	actual number	257	465

Source: *Joshi Kôtô Kyôiku no Zahyô*, 1986.

a survey focusing on female college students from all over Japan in 1972 had the same results (Amano, 1986).

Because of mass education, it was common to accept students who didn't have a clear purpose in mind. Under such circumstances, notions that female students might destroy the nation and that the college didn't like accepting female students were discussed in some magazines at that time. An icebreaker was Mr. Teruoka Yasutaka, a professor in the literature department of Waseda Daigaku, one of the famous coed private schools in Japan. He said in *Fujin Kôron*, "Before 1955, most of the female students in Waseda Daigaku were pioneers who covered various fields. When I gave those students interviews as part of their entrance exams, they all had clear purposes for obtaining a higher education and strong intentions to contribute to society. However, nowadays, even if I ask female students their purposes for studying at college, most of them answer without hesitation that they have nothing in particular in mind. Moreover, they say they don't have to work after graduation. They still have four or five years before marriage at hand and they want to obtain broad general knowledge in college. (At that time the average marriage age was 22 or 23 in Japan.) Because generally, female students study more seriously than males, their scores of entrance exams were better than those of male students. For this reason, male students, who were going to have an outside job as a career and become main foundations of support to the Japanese nation, were shut out of Waseda Daigaku, while female students who were going to marry early and let go of outside jobs went to study there. More than half of all students in the literature department of Waseda Daigaku are women and this number is definitely going to increase. This situation will contribute to avoiding the development of the Japanese country and may destroy it in the future. Before World War II, no one imagined this situation." (Teruoka,

1962, March).

Mr. Teruoka also pointed out his opinion in *Shûkan Asahi* three months later. He described, "There are still many young men who can't afford to go to college, even if they have enough talent. Because students who are allowed to spend a lot of money for a college education are a select people, they need to have duties to return what they learned there back to society. If female students study hard in college and find occupations to contribute to society, it is fine. However, most of their final goals are to become wives without outside jobs. Even if they engage in occupations, they will quit soon after marriage. It is more important for the college to foster male students who will surely contribute to society even if their scores in examinations are not so good. College is not a finishing school to prepare the middle and upper class women for marriage" (Teruoka, 1962, June 29).

According to Ogawa (1967, May 7), drug courses in pharmaceutical departments at some national universities such as Kumamoto Daigaku, Osaka Daigaku and Kyushu Daigaku were occupied by female students. In 1967, only one male student was accepted by Kyushu Daigaku and no male students were allowed to enter in both Kumamoto Daigaku and Osaka Daigaku. As far as Kumamoto Daigaku, after 165 female students and 11 male students tried the entrance examination for this course, only 43 female students were accepted in 1967. In 1966, only two male students were accepted for this course while 42 female students made it. This university isn't keen on increasing the number of female students. As Kumamoto Daigaku mentioned, "Good female students have increased year by year so that finally this course has no male students this year. Because male students in other grades were very few, they were usually studying at the corner of the classroom while female students were learning in the center of class freely. The problem with having female students is that many students don't use their certificates of pharmacy after their graduation. This means one-third of students obtaining these certificates don't engage in occupations. They see these certificates as simply one degree closer towards their marriage. Because most of the female students have no intention of going to graduate school to pursue further study, it is very difficult to find successors. Even if they do go to graduate school, almost four years later they quit because of their marriages. This is a problem not for one institution but for society."

The same thing was pointed out by Mr. Okuno Shintarô, a professor of the literature department in Wasada Daigaku. He said, "In old times many good educators for high schools and colleges were fostered in the literature department, while nowadays, it is difficult to keep such human resources. Even though female students have talents they don't return to society" (*Josei Jishin*, 1966, July 25).

Mr. Ikeda Yosaburô, a professor of the literature department at Keiôgijuku Daigaku, which is also one of the most famous private coed schools in Japan, made the point that his school didn't want to accept many female students. Ikeda (1962, April) put it this way: "Because parents are less passionate about their daughters' education than their sons', the parents of female students don't donate a lot of money to their daughters' schools. Female students also don't donate much money after their graduation because most of them don't have occupations. Furthermore, after marriage, they forget about their school and never return to contribute anything, even though the faculties trained them for four years. On the other hand, the school can expect male students to contribute after their graduation. A donation issue is very important for private institutions. Without financial aid from graduates it is impossible for private schools to continue. Female students may bring financial problems to this school.

After 1955, when the Japanese economy recovered, people began to take back their lives, and the ideas of equality between men and women and women's emancipation and improvement, born after World War II, were getting unpopular. Instead, the backlash idea that women should return to domestic work because it is their mission in life began to be spread around. This was another reason for discussing this matter. The idea that women should stay home and men should go outside to work was encouraged further by the education policy of the Japanese government. Because education considering women's 'natures' was emphasized, to focus only on the importance of keeping a family, the Ministry of Education in Japan announced reformed curriculums for elementary and middle schools. The contents of them were to include sewing and knitting in girls' curriculums while subjects to learn skills and gymnastics were added into boys'. This new policy was started in 1961 for elementary schools and in 1962 for middle schools (Murakami, 1959, February 8). This policy originated from the old idea of a good wife and wise mother based on Japanese Confucianism (Aoki, 1995).

The tendency of Japanese society in the late 1960s, through the 1970s, was that women from the middle and upper classes married after working outside the home for three or four years following the finishing of their higher education for two or four years. In particular, private women's junior colleges became very popular after 1964 when the junior college system became permanent. After a lot of private women's junior colleges were established, many female students came to study there. After the woman graduated from a women's junior college and found work in a big company, she found an elite businessman graduating from a four-year college to marry there. Here was one reason someone said that the women's junior college was the preparation school for women's marriage. After marrying, she became a housewife without an outside job, engaging in every kind of domestic work and taking care of children and her husband who worked overtime every day in the company, thus contributing 'big time' to developing the country. It was the big dream for the young woman from higher education in those days to live in a house in the suburbs as the elite businessman's wife (Yasukawa, 1996 January). This type of lifestyle in Japan was solidified in the middle of a period of high economic growth in the country, and Japanese men were called 'economic animals' in the world.

Because of this lifestyle, private women's junior colleges with home economics courses became popular among young women because most of the national and public junior colleges didn't have this course. The meaning of home economics in Japan in 1970 was an actual and practical science contributing to improving the lives of individuals at home, leading to human beings' happiness, by studying the relationships between people's lives at home, social events and their environment physically and materialistically (Handa, 1986). Actually, the subjects offered in the course at women's junior colleges in those days were associated with domestic work, including mainly housekeeping, food (cooking) and clothes (sewing), which were not so different from those offered in *kôtô jogakkô* before World War II. Many people thought that home economics was a course for women and that there were almost no coed four-year colleges which had home economics courses (except a few) all over Japan. We can understand people's impression toward home economics then from Table 24: the need for studying home economics. The percentage of women who should learn home economics and women whose majors are home economics was over 50% in both junior colleges and four-year colleges, while the percentage of both male and female students who should study

Table 24 : The need for studying home economics
A: Both male and female students should study home economics in junior colleges and colleges.
B: Only female students should learn home economics.
C-1: Female students whose majors are home economics should study home economics.
C-2: Male students whose majors are home economics should study home economics.
D: Male students don't have to learn home economics.
E: No answer.

	colleges			junior colleges		
	female	male	total	female	male	total
A	6	2	8(11.9%)	4	1	5(3.3%)
B	6	5	11(16.4%)	19	12	31(20.7%)
C-1	10	14	24(35.8%)	31	29	60(40.0%)
C-2	5	7	12(17.9%)	31	18	49(32.7%)
D	1	1	2(3.0%)	0	1	1(0.6%)
E	5	5	10(14.9%)	2	2	4(2.6%)
Total	33	34	67(100%)	87	63	150(100.0)

Source: *Joshi Kôtô Kyôiku no Zahyô*, 1986.

home economics was 11.9% in four-year colleges and 3.3% in junior colleges. Here there was still the old concept that women should learn home economics because they engaged in domestic work after their marriage, which presented a traditional women's sex role.

In addition to home economics, courses related to education which students could take to obtain qualifications for kindergarten and nursery teaching were set up, becoming popular in the 1970s. This indicated that the function of private women's junior colleges came to be not only training future housewives but also training women with qualifications for outside occupations. This meant that women from junior colleges now had job qualifications which would help her family with a financial problem in addition to being ready as good wives. In 1984, 43% of all junior colleges were allowed

Table 25 : The number of schools which offer qualifications

qualifications	national	public	private
kindergarten teacher	0	16	214
nursery teacher	0	16	205
clothing managers	0	0	30
dietitian	0	19	131
secretary	0	0	73
librarian	0	0	83

Source: *Joshi Kôtô Kyôiku no Zahyô*, 1986.

to offer qualifications for kindergarten teacher and 41% of them could qualify as nursery teacher. The home economics course also offered qualifications for dietitian and clothing managers. However, there were no national junior colleges which offered these qualifications in Japan (Kameda, 1986). Table 25 shows that graduates of private women's junior colleges contributed very much to these fields.

In the 1990s, women's junior colleges could offer some further qualifications related to education. There were qualifications for elementary teacher, teacher for disabled children and middle school teacher (Yamamoto, 1995). Almost every subject's qualification for middle school could be obtained in junior colleges. Table 26 describes what subjects' qualifications in middle schools were popular among students in 1994. This data was collected by 220 junior colleges which were 59% of all total institutions offering the qualifications of middle school teachers. The percentage of those obtaining teacher's qualifications for physical education was the largest number, 60.7% of students learning this subject. The percentage of those getting teacher's qualifications in music was the second largest number. Though 91 schools offered qualifications for teaching English and 18,283 students majored in English, only 7.5% of these obtained teachers' qualifications. This meant that, because English was useful for various other

Table 26 : Those obtaining teaching qualifications for middle school
1. the number of schools
2. the number of students learning the subject
3. the number of students obtaining teaching qualifications in the subject
4. percentage of students obtaining teaching qualifications

	1	2	3	4
home economics	96	17,209	1,714	10.0%
English	91	18,283	1,379	7.5%
Japanese literature	60	8,816	1,103	12.5%
music	24	1,966	1,118	56.9%
health	18	3,053	516	16.9%
fine arts	17	3,148	267	8.5%
physical education	3	521	316	60.7%
social science	22	3,195	184	5.8%
math	1	192	24	12.5%
science	4	702	4	0.6%
religion	3	340	13	3.8%
vocation	1	100	12	12.0%
other skills	2	710	25	3.5%

Source: *Wayô Joshi Daigaku Kiyô*, 1995.

fields such as business, becoming an English teacher was not the only way to use what they learned.

The secretarial course was also introduced in many women's junior colleges in 1980 when the Ministry of Education in Japan permitted them to establish this course. In 1982, the secretarial course began to be offered in each junior college. The purpose of this course was to train experts with knowledge and skills needed by companies and enterprises. In 1992, Zenkoku Tanki Daigaku Hisho Kyôiku Kyôkai (The association of secretarial education by the junior colleges all over Japan) set up curriculums to earn advanced secretarial qualifications as well as the regular kind. Regarding the curriculum for the advanced secretarial course, the students had to take more than 20 credits from the required subjects to include these: general outline for the secretary, introduction to business administration, theories of human relationships, global understanding, language and expression, the business secretary, Japanese language expression, office management, a foreign language and a seminar for using office tools. They also had to take more than 20 credits from those elective subjects that were permitted by Zenkoku Tanki Daigaku Hisho Kyôiku Kyôkai. The number of these credits for the advanced secretarial course was equal to two times that of the regular secretarial course. The aims of these secretarial courses were: 1. To offer education to prepare for occupations. 2. To train people of good personal character. 3. To help students have open minds to global affairs, and 4. To offer education which would cover life learning in society (Shibayama, 1993). Because of these increasing secretarial courses, other courses related to the secretarial component such as law, business and economics began to be set up in women's junior colleges as well (Kameda, 1986).

As the policy of women's junior colleges changed from at first simply offering general knowledge, to then offering educational courses for qualification during the 1970s and 1980s, the purposes of students with junior college education also changed. According to Table 22, speaking of the purpose of going to higher education among female students, having general knowledge was the highest, or 38% for female junior college students in 1958. On the other hand, Table 27 mentioned that obtaining qualifications got the highest mark, 35% among female junior college students. The second highest mark was professional education, at 31.1% and obtaining general knowledge was third place at 17% (Hirasawa, 1991). This tendency in women's junior colleges will continue for a while because there are many women working outside the home since the middle of the 1990s when the Japanese economy went down.

Table 27 : The purpose for entering junior colleges

to obtain qualifications	35%
to get a degree	17%
to have general knowledge	17%
to get professional education	31%
total	100%

Source: *Soshioroji*, 1991.

A growing problem for students in these junior colleges was that they were so busy earning qualifications that they had hardly any time to enjoy their school lives and to think deeply about their futures. In order to gain qualifications they had to take extra credits in addition to the required credits for the liberal arts classes. Because some students tried to achieve multiple qualifications, their school lives were very busy. We can understand this situation from Table 28–a and Table 28–b. Table 28–a was the survey which was carried out in 1999 focusing on the second year students in a women's junior college (Hayashi et al., 2001). 42.7% of all students answered 'graduation' for the question of, 'What is the most important thing for you in your school life?' and 'to do something only I can do' had the second largest percentage, 23.9%. Table 28–b was the information from junior college students at Osaka Jogakuin College in 2009. Here, 'graduation' also had the largest percentage. Because in most of the junior colleges, getting qualifications was one of the requirements for graduation, it seemed 'status quo' that they couldn't do anything else except study to obtain them, in spite of the desire to do something only they could do. As a consequence, they had almost no time to spend on extracurricular activities like a club or circle activities, and no time for concerns about family. In short, studying for two years in junior college didn't give most of the students enough time to consider their families or try to discover new lives to de-

Table 28–a : What is the most important thing in your school life?

professional education	4.0%
graduation	42.7%
club and circle activities	2.0%
part time job	0.8%
friendships	9.3%
general knowledge	6.4%
doing something only one can do	23.9%
family	0.4%
enjoying everyday life	7.7%
others	2.5%
no answer	0.4%

Source: *Wayô Joshi Daigaku Kiyô*, 2001.

Table 28–b: What is the most important thing in your school life?

professional education	9.0%
graduation	45.5%
club and circle activities	0%
friendship	18.2%
general knowledge	9.1%
doing something only one can do	23.9%
family	0%
others	18.2%

(Students could choose more than one answer.)
Source: Osaka Jogakuin College in 2009.

velop themselves.

Another problem in private junior colleges was a lack of full-time instructors. Table 29 talks about the number of students (both male and female) and the number of full-time instructors in all junior colleges. Because more than 90% of all students in junior colleges were studying in private institutions and almost 90% of them were women, this problem was most serious for women's higher education. Until 1995, in national and public schools, the number of students per instructor was 12 or 13 on average while it was 25 on average in private schools (The Ministry of Education in Japan, 1976, 1986, 1996, and 2001; The Ministry of Education, Culture, Sports, and Technology in Japan, 2006 and 2011). After 1995, the situation became a little better but it is still not so good. There were reasons for this: 1. They didn't hire enough full-time instructors because their financial situations were not good. Most of the private junior colleges were small in size and the numbers of students on average were about 700 per school. In addition, the Ministry of Education hadn't provided enough money for junior colleges since it didn't see them as significant research institutions. 2. The criteria to accepting part-time instructors is not so strict. Because they offer more subjects than regular colleges, in order to offer up the qualifications, they need various types of part-time instructors (Matsumura, 1984). Two-thirds of all instructors in the junior colleges are part-time instructors (The Ministry of Education, 1986 and 2001). As the part-time instructors don't have to involve themselves in school affairs directly except for teaching their subjects, the lack of full-time instructors makes it difficult for junior colleges to provide enough appropriate educational atmosphere for their students as a whole.

Private women's four-year colleges also contributed to women's higher education in Japan because there were only two national and six public women's colleges in the entire country. 99% of all women's colleges were private. One of the advantages of women's colleges was that they had a lot of female personnel and faculty who helped female students cultivate themselves as good female models (Matsusawa, 2000). Almost 40% of all personnel and faculty in women's colleges were women (Tanioka, 2000). Furthermore, female students developed their own leadership because the absence

Table 29 : The number of students (both male & female) and the number of full-time instructors in junior colleges

	National			Public			Private		
	the number of students	the number of full-time instructors	the number of students per instructor	the number of students	the number of full-time instructors	the number of students per instructor	the number of students	the number of full-time instructors	the number of students per instructor
1975	13,143	654	21	17,973	1,617	12	322,666	13,286	25
1985	17,530	1,121	12	20,767	1,898	11	332,798	14,741	23
1995	13,735	1,122	12	24,134	2,219	10	460,647	17,381	26
2000	7,772	713	10	21,061	1,863	11	298,847	14,176	21
2005	1,643	244	6	14,347	1,209	11	203,365	10,507	19
2010	0	0	0	9,128	692	13	146,145	8,965	16

Source: *Gakkō Kihon Chōsa Hōkokusho*, 1976, 1986, 1996, 2001, 2006 and 2011.

of male competition was a significant factor in seeking leadership positions. Women's colleges provided them with many chances and positions to be seen as central and to be present in diverse roles. Female students also trained in interactive leadership which stemmed from women's natural nurturing and caring sensibilities. This was far different from the functional leadership being exercised among men. Female sensitivities could be developed among women because they shared power and information while enhancing other people's self-worth and all of this emphasized the value of collaboration to achieve goals which promoted their self-esteem as well. Once they had confidence, it helped them to work at anything more forcefully, which led to better results.

However, the purpose of going to women's colleges was not to receive the advantages mentioned above but to obtain general knowledge. Table 30-a describes the purpose of entering women's college, which was presented by female students in five women's colleges (A, B, C, D and E) in Nagoya Prefecture, Japan, in the 1990s. Obtaining general knowledge was 27.4% of the objective, the highest percentage of all and the next was getting qualifications, which was 20% (Tsuzuki & Takamori, 1993).

Regarding Table 30-b containing information from Osaka Jogakuin College, obtaining general knowledge took 43.8% which was also the highest percentage of all and the next was finding a better job at 37.5%. Others had 18.2%, which included entertainment such as enjoying school life. (Because students could choose multiple answers, the total number was more than 100%.) When comparing Table 30-a 1993 and Table 30-b, 2009 with Table 22, 1958 and Table 23, 1986, we recognized that the female student's purpose of going to women's higher education had not changed very much since World War II. From this result, we may surmise that those living the college life seemed to enjoy their lives,

Table 30-a : The purpose of entering women's college
1. study and do research
2. find a better job
3. obtain general knowledge
4. get qualifications
5. because many people go to higher education nowadays
6. because the parent expected them to go to higher education
7. enjoy school life
8. others

%

	A	B	C	D	E	average
1	11	6	9	13	6	8.6
2	12	6	12	15	7	10.4
3	28	26	31	27	25	27.4
4	19	44	8	15	14	20
5	9	11	7	4	1	6.4
6	0.5	1	8	3	11	4.7
7	18	22	19	15	21	19
8	4	6	3	6	6	5

Source: *Sugiyama Jogakuin Daigaku Kenkyûronshû*, 1993.

Table 30-b: The purpose of entering women's college

to get professional education	31.3%
to obtain general knowlegde	43.8%
to make friends	6.3%
to find a better job	37.5%
for a better marriage	12.5%
because many people go to higher education nowadays	25.0%
others	18.2%

Source: Osaka Jogakuin College in 2009.

absorbing general knowledge.

Choosing a women's college was not only the students' decision themselves but also their parent's decision. In Japan, 70% of all women's colleges had attached girls' high schools and 60% of the girls' high schools had attached girls' middle schools. Because students in attached girls' middle schools had priority to go to the high schools and colleges within the same schools, they didn't have to study so hard to go to high school and college. Since entrance examinations for every level were difficult in Japan, the parents chose this route for their daughters so that they wouldn't have to compete with other students. The decision in choosing a middle school was usually influenced by the parent's opinions because the students were too young to decide which school was appropriate for them. The values of these parents who sent their daughters to girls' middle schools and high schools that had women's colleges as extensions were different from those parents who sent their daughters to coed colleges. The parents sending their daughters to such women's colleges had the idea that separate education was better for girls, not expecting to have their daughters earn professional education which would contribute to finding a good job and get a high social position or to become a scholar in a higher education institution but to help them obtain womanly knowledge and sense that was fostered only in women's colleges. These parents' ways of thinking were also related to the idea that women's social position was decided by marriage as well as the occupation. They still thought that a woman's marriage decided her social position more than her occupation. It was not always a woman's ideal for these parents that she should engage in an occupation competing with other men. Instead, they aimed at training the calm and quiet woman with the ability to make a home environment comfortable. Here, the traditional idea of a good wife and wise mother still seemed to exist.

Some changes occurred within women's junior and four-year colleges in order to attract students because the number of 18-year-olds decreased after 1992. They changed the name of the home economics department to life course, life culture, life science, etc., by changing the content of subjects they offered. Because of the unpopularity of home economics, in 1986 the Ministry of Education in Japan permitted a policy of changing its name and contents (Mori, 1991a). Ochanomizu Joshi Daigaku changed the name of the home economics department to the life science department in 1992 and Nara Joshi Daigaku changed theirs to the life environment department in 1993 (Ôishi et al., 2000). The primary subjects offered in this new course or department were life introduction, theories of clothing life, food life, residence life, life administration and life history which helped to find connections between life at home and a person's social economics, including internships associated with social welfare such as volunteer activities (Mori, 1991a). Some schools offered new qualifications related to clothing management and residence specialists such as color coordinator, kitchen specialist and interior coordinator.

Some schools were changed from women's schools to coed schools. By 1999, 27 women's colleges became coed with almost half of them changed after 1990. 57.4% of all women's junior colleges that were changed into coed schools did so after 1990, especially after 1997. These schools also established new departments which were pharmacy, dentist, economics and business administration for male students because most of the women's schools had only home economics and literature departments. These changes mainly occurred in local areas while in big cities like Tokyo, such changes were not common (Okada, 1999). After a school became coed, the number of entering students increased and a vigorous atmosphere was born on campus. For example, club or circle activities were active and many students participated in school festivals. Students now tried to do things spontaneously without depending on school and study associated with their interests.

After the 1980s, students tended to choose coed schools.

In the 1990s, many women's schools set up new departments fitting students' and social needs. They also tried to offer courses which contributed to training women to improve themselves and to change male-oriented society by casting off the idea of developing good wives and wise mothers so that cooperation between men and women could establish a more healthy and cultivated society.

However, after 2000 many women's colleges were absorbed by other schools or closed because of lack of students. According to Table 9 (p.117), the number of female colleges (universities) was 97 in 2000 and only 81 in 2010. As far as the number of female junior colleges (Table 10, p.118), the situation was worse. In 2000 there were 252 female junior colleges but only 122 in 2010. Women's colleges and junior colleges need new policies and plans to attract new students in order to survive in the future.

5) Occupations

Once the doors opened after World War II for women to have a chance at a higher education, they took full advantage of their opportunities, and by 1951, 85.6% of all female students graduating from four-year colleges obtained jobs just after graduation (Table 31, p.159). When compared with the percentages for getting jobs of middle school graduates, high school graduates and junior college graduates (45.8%, 37.5% and 48.3% respectively), this number was much higher than those for women with lesser educations. Higher education certainly seemed to contribute to women's obtaining jobs. However, this high percentage of college graduates employed decreased to 67.5% in 1955 and this decrease in percentage continued after that year (The Ministry of Education in Japan, 2001).

The first reason why it decreased was a tremendous increase in the number of students finishing higher education from around 1955 and there were not enough occupations to accept all the female students in spite of their higher achievements. As for jobs in the special fields, there was little possibility of expanding opportunities even with economic growth. For example, the demand for teachers depended on the number of children of school age. This was related to the rate of birth. Women trying to find a job in this field found it to be very competitive not only among the women but also with men finishing higher education and so it would be more difficult for female students with higher education to get positions (Amano, 1986).

Table 32 (p.159) and Table 33 (p.160) describe the situation of occupations for women having four-year college and junior college degrees. Although most of these women with higher education had engaged in special or technical jobs such as technical experts, teachers, those engaged in health and medical fields, and even artists before World War II and just after, the rate of employment in the special or technical fields decreased and that of employment for office work in companies increased due to the Japanese economic situation. For instance, in 1955, out of 9,143 graduates obtaining jobs, 7,674 (84%) of four-year college female students got jobs in the special or technical fields, and 1,044 (11%) of them engaged in office work. In the same year, 4,127 out of 6,598 (63%) of junior college female students received their jobs in special or technical fields, while 1,918 (29%) of them were doing office work. In 1965, for four-year college female students, out of 17,528 who found jobs, 12,525 (71%) of them still found their positions of employ in special or technical fields, while 3,657 (21%) of them did office work. In the same year, with junior college female students, out of 24,354 who got jobs, some 10,145 (42%) of them worked in special or technical fields and 11,624 (48%) of them were engaged in office work. Around this time, junior college female students were already beginning to find more job opportunities in office work than in special or technical fields. Although more than 50% of the four-year college students still found jobs in special or technical fields over time, this situation gradually changed. In 1995, out of 101,278 four-year college graduates who found jobs, 30,447 of them (30%) were engaged in special or technical fields while 49,922 (49%) worked in office work. In 2007, four-year college graduates also found more jobs in office work than in special or technical fields. However, junior college female graduates obtained more jobs in special or technical fields than in office work because many junior colleges began to offer qualifications to help them become specialists since the 1970s.

The second reason why the number of women with four-year college degrees who were engaged in jobs decreased after 1955 was that attitudes in Japanese society at that time had changed. The idea that men should be outside workers and that women belonged inside to do the homemaking came back in vogue. For this reason, generally female students with higher education around after 1955 didn't try to seek jobs so strongly, although there were some exceptions, as compared with women with higher education before 1955. A person working in a career services center at a college said, "There were many male students who tried job positions 20 times or more to get jobs while female students did at most only a few times. Moreover, a lot of parents having sons are very positive about their sons' job hunt, on the other hand most of the parents having daughters don't pay much attention to that of their daughters" (*Fujin Kôron*, 1957, December).

Regarding private enterprises, most of them, especially the big companies, actually did not invite female students with four-year college degrees except as broadcasters and translators until the 1980s and then only some middle and small companies did (Takahara, 1964, September). Even if female students got a job in a big company because of special connections, their treatment was not so different from that of women finishing high school and their salaries also didn't fit their educational backgrounds (Murakami, 1959, February 8).

The reasons why these companies did not invite women finishing four-year colleges were explained this way. Everyone knew that because the Japanese Constitution permitted equality between men and women, women should be accepted based on the same conditions as men. However, women's ability to complete their work was lower than those of men. Though they worked seriously, they lacked the abilities of decision, creativity and leadership (Tsuchiya, 1956, February). What's more, since women didn't take strong responsibilities for supporting their family economically, their attitudes to work were not serious and they usually quit their jobs three or four years after they were employed because of marriage. Even if the company educated their women employees on the job to do their work at a higher level of achievement, all such effort would be lost when they left. Enterprises were not non-profit organizations. As long as they needed to pursue their profits, they didn't want to hire female students who wouldn't contribute to the companies over time. In addition, most of them took extended vacation time to give birth to a baby, didn't like to be transferred and had reservations about working late (Takahara, 1964, September). Then too, why female students wanted jobs was not clear. Companies didn't want to accept the female students if their purposes were just to get some money for entertainment before marriage and find future husbands (Tsuchiya, 1956, February). It was not enough for female students just to finish higher education in order to get jobs in those days because many women had college degrees. They needed to become specialists in their work, having something only that person could do and do their best in (*Bungei Shunjû*, 1965, September).

Against these opinions, some female students who were seriously looking for jobs are mentioned in the following. Although enterprises said that women with four-year college degrees lacked ability in terms of various fields, actually they were not offered enough education associated with the jobs as were men finishing their four-year college work. This meant that from the beginning, enterprises had no intention of training women to work on mainline jobs and simply did not expect them to contribute very much to increasing the profit of the companies. Women held assistant positions, helping men and their main job was making tea. Sometimes they needed to go outside to buy tobacco for their boss. These were dead-end jobs and women were not allowed to accumulate career advantages. Not every female student's purpose for engaging in jobs was to get money for entertainment before marriage and find their future husbands. Some female students had strong passions for their jobs. It was the company's responsibility to find good female workers with acute insights. Although there were complaints that women quit their jobs after marriage and at most worked only three or four years after being hired, it was very difficult to do both outside and domestic jobs perfectly so long as men depended 100 percent on their wives to do domestic work (*Fujin Kôron*, 1957, December).

Here are some explanations about company policy in Japan then and now. Most of the Japanese corporations had traditionally accepted the system of lifetime employment. This protective employment system gradually became insecure beginning around 1992 when the Japanese economic downturn began. Before then, once employees were engaged in a company, they were trained and educated by their companies in order to fit their companies' needs. In Japan, the relationship between job descriptions and subjects students learned in school was not exactly connected, and one's educational background didn't qualify a worker to be able to fill a special job but only meant that one's potential ability, how much one could contribute to his or her company's needs in the future, was the factor in question (Nihon Joshi Daigaku Joshi Kyôiku Kenkyûsho, 1987). For this reason, people graduating even from higher institutions found it difficult to contribute to their companies so soon. Usually it took four to five years to do so after they were engaged in their jobs. Because of this, many enterprises in Japan didn't want to hire women who were going to quit their jobs in three–four years.

According to Table 31, around 1975 women with junior college degrees had the highest percentage of all women being hired. It meant, especially in private enterprises, that women finishing junior colleges took precedence over women with high school degrees because the number of women with junior college degrees increased and enhanced ability to deal with more complicated work at a higher-level of achievement was required following Japanese high economic growth. However, most of the enterprises still didn't accept women from four-year colleges. The reasons were: 1. Because the wage system was based on the employee's age (which meant the older employee could get more money than the younger one), the enterprises had to pay more money for women with four-year college degrees than for women with junior college degrees, 2. The working period for women finishing four-year college was generally shorter than that for women completing junior college and a shorter working period didn't contribute to the enterprise's bottom line, and 3. Though the content of work was more complicated and required higher-level technique and knowledge, it didn't need a college women's special knowledge and techniques (Nihon Rikurûto Sentâ Kikaku Chôsashitsu Chôsaka, 1980). So even if women with four-year college degrees were engaged, their jobs were not so different from those of women with junior college degrees and all their jobs were peripheral ones, not like the mainstream ones given to men. Then too, the salary gap between women from four-year colleges and those from junior colleges was very small (Tanaka & Nishimura, 1986). Conditions for women coming from junior colleges were better than those for women from four-year colleges when their educational backgrounds were considered and compared.

It was 1986 when the Ordinance of Equal Opportunities in Occupations between men and women was established by the Japanese government and at that time the situation for women with four-year college degrees in the enterprises

Table 31 : Percentage of women engaging in occupations

%

	middle school	high school	junior college	four year college	master	doctor
1951	45.8	37.5	48.3	85.6	0	0
1955	40.9	38.6	42.5	67.5	41.8	0
1960	37.5	58.6	49.8	64.1	32.9	0
1965	26.0	62.9	57.4	66.7	32.4	41.4
1970	16.1	61.2	68.8	59.9	37.1	51.7
1975	5.9	48.0	73.0	62.8	36.0	53.6
1980	3.2	45.6	76.4	65.7	36.2	40.0
1985	2.9	43.4	81.3	72.4	44.3	50.8
1990	1.8	36.2	88.1	81.0	49.6	48.4
1995	0.9	23.4	66.0	63.7	46.6	50.0
2000	0.5	16.5	57.4	57.1	46.6	45.2
2005	0.4	14.9	66.8	64.1	55.2	49.8
2010	0.2	13.1	67.3	66.6	60.7	53.2

Source: *Monbu Tôkei Yôran*, 2001 and *Monbu Kagaku Tôkei Yôran*, 2011.

Table 32 : The situation concerning occupations for college female students

	special & technical job	office work	sales	others	total
1955	7,674	1,044	105	320	9,143
1965	12,525	3,657	225	1,121	17,528
1975	22,369	17,152	1,302	1,614	42,437
1985	33,747	26,149	5,230	1,764	66,890
1995	30,447	49,922	14,660	6,249	101,278
2007	53,570	67,834	34,269	17,104	172,777

changed (LY, 1998). Before 1986, for instance, in a big trading company there were three types of positions: an executive one, a general one and office work. The general positions were the pathways to the executive ones and were for men finishing four-year colleges, while office work (assistant positions to help the men in general positions and not in them-

Table 33 : The situation concerning occupations for junior college female students

	special & technical job	office work	sales	others	total
1955	4,127	1,918	132	421	6,598
1965	10,145	11,624	930	1,655	24,354
1975	35,289	50,026	2,148	3,858	91,321
1985	38,886	80,891	7,876	4,095	131,748
1995	40,066	83,281	16,869	10,710	150,926
2007	32,669	14,769	6,670	4,683	58,791

Table 34 : The situation concerning occupations for female Masters students

	special & technical job	office work	sales	others	total
1965	110	3	0	8	121
1975	361	26	3	51	339
1985	929	109	10	29	1,077
1995	2,806	622	39	210	3,677
2007	9,380	2,295	443	1,298	13,416

This doesn't include students working in professional degree courses in graduate schools.

Table 35 : The situation concerning occupations for female Doctoral students

	special & technical job	office work	sales	others	total
1965	48	0	0	0	48
1975	88	0	0	2	90
1985	211	3	0	4	218
1995	585	15	1	23	624
2007	2,100	71	2	97	2,270

The above doesn't include students working in professional degree courses in graduate schools.
Sources: *Gakkô Kihon Chôsa Hôkokusho*, 1956, 1966 and 1976.
Monbu Tôkei Yôran, 1986, 1996 and *Monbu Kagaku Tôkei Yôran*, 2008.

selves the route to executive positions in the future) was for the women with higher education. For this reason, the pay of women finishing four-year colleges was less than that for the men finishing four-year colleges (Tanaka & Nishimura, 1986). However, because of the Ordinance in 1986, women finishing four-year colleges were allowed wherever the opportunity presented itself to get general positions and eventually executive positions if they were capable (LY, 1998).

According to Table 31, the percentage of engaging in occupations for women with four-year college degrees in 1990 was 81%, the highest ratio after 1955. Because of the Ordinance of Equal Opportunities in Occupations in 1986 and a good Japanese economic situation based on the inflated (i.e.: bubble) economy at that time, a lot of enterprises invited female workers in with four-year college degrees (Kaneko, 1995). An elective system was introduced into especially big companies and women finishing four-year colleges could choose either a general position with transfer possibilities for advancement or office work which didn't require transfer possibilities when entering the company (Yasui, 2001). Many enterprises began to open up general jobs from the beginning to women with four-year college degrees and expectations about women in such enterprises seemed to be raised.

Around 1993 women's employment opportunities decreased dramatically because of the Japanese economic downturn. People called this time the 'ultra frozen period' and it was a serious social problem as well (Môri, 1999, April). The percentage of women obtaining jobs was 75.6% out of the women who graduated from four-year colleges in 1993, 67.6% in 1994 and 63.7% in 1995. These numbers kept decreasing year by year while the employment gap between men and women became bigger and bigger (*The Yomiuri Shimbun*, 1995, November 7).

In addition, according to *Osaka Asahi Shimbun* (1999,

May 24), because of the 1986 Ordinance, many enterprises in Japan did invite women to apply but they could not accept them into their work force because of the continuing economic depression. When a survey asked a thousand enterprises about equal opportunities in occupations between men and women, 27.7% of them said that it was difficult if not impossible to achieve it. While this ordinance was needed to help women in general, they still had a hard time finding a job. With less and less jobs available for more and more applicants, the ordinance clearly could not work at all.

Where promotions were concerned, men usually became section chiefs between 35–39 years of age, a division chief between 45–49, and department chief by 50–54 years and their promotions went on smoothly. On the other hand, female workers usually reached section chief and division chief when they were 45–49 years old. The highest number of promotions were to section chief; the number of department chiefs was small by comparison (The Ministry of Labor in Japan, 1995). The Ministry of Labor, Health, and Welfare in Japan (2007) said that only 8.8% of all department chiefs whose companies were 66.6% of all companies in Japan were women, 21.2% of all division chiefs and 32% of all section chiefs were females in 2006. According to Bandô in *The Yomiuri Shimbun* (2011, July 27), the number of female executives in enterprises was still small.

The main reasons why the number of female executives in enterprises was small were as follows: 1. There were no female personnel having enough knowledge, experience and decision-making capabilities required, 2. Most of the female personnel hadn't worked at the company for a long time or they retired before reaching executive consideration, and 3. Although there were some female workers with the potential to progress to executive positions in the future, their present work experiences were not enough (The Ministry of Labor in

Japan, 2000; The Ministry of Health, Labor, and Welfare in Japan, 2007).

There was a survey talking about how long women with higher education were going to continue their jobs after graduation. It was answered by both junior college and college students in Osaka Jogakuin College in 2009. 18.5% of all the students said that they were not going to keep their jobs after graduation while 81.5% of them answered that they were going to keep their jobs. According to Table 36, 31.8% out of the 81.5% people told us that they were going to work until marriage and 4.5% of those persons mentioned they were going to work until having a baby. 68.2% students hoped that they could start working again after finishing taking care of their children although they quit their jobs after having their babies. No participants reported that they would continue their jobs throughout life.

The reason so many women quit jobs so soon before receiving executive levels should be focused on. There were problems preventing women from continuing their jobs. The biggest problem was that the Japanese company's system of covering both outside jobs and domestic work, especially taking care of children and old sick parents, was not enough. (In Japan, it is still the habit for the elderly to be taken care of by their children's family.) Others were: 1. Because the job world was still a man's society, there were some atmospheres not acceptable to female workers. Though the rule that women had to quit their jobs after marriage and deliver-

Table 36 : How long are you going to continue your job after graduation?

until marriage	31.8%
until having a ababy	4.5%
after having a baby, quit a job but become reemployed after completing childcare	68.2%
continue employment	0%

ing a baby was abolished because of the 1986 Ordinance, some companies still habitually felt that female workers should give up their jobs after their marriage and deliveries. There were no working women who were married or had children in 20% of all companies in Japan. 2. Because there was a lot of overtime work, the employees had almost no private time (The Ministry of Labor in Japan, 2000).

What kind of surroundings would help women cover both their outside positions and domestic work, especially taking care of their children? Some married women with general positions thought that it would not be difficult for them to take holidays from the office to be with their children if their working time was flexible, and if they didn't have to overwork. Regarding family support, most would live with their parents who could look after their children or their parents would live close to their house and at any time they could ask their parents to look in or help out in some way (Morita, 2000). Because in Japan facilities like child-care centers are not popular, such systems would not be enough to answer their requirements. Without family help it would be almost impossible for women with jobs to bring up their children.

The Ministry of Health, Labor and Welfare in Japan (2009) told us about how the working percentage of women with higher education has changed. When women with higher education were between 20–24 years old, more than 90% of women who wanted to have jobs found them after graduation and were working. This number gradually decreased as their ages increased. When they became 35–39 years old, this percentage decreased to 65.8% which was the smallest number. This number gradually increased a little to 73.4% when they were 45–49 years old. After that, this number gradually decreased again. The reason why this number decreased to 65.8% when they were 35–59 was that they quit their jobs due to taking care of their children. In Japan, most of the women graduated from their colleges when they were 22 years old. The average age of their first marriage was when they were 28.23 years old. At about the age of 30, most of them had their first child, with their second child when they were 32 or 33. When they were about 40 years old, their youngest children went to elementary schools. Because of this average lifestyle, most of the women who wanted to get work again came back after they were 40 years of age. Actually, most of the women who had had jobs before delivering their children never did get their old jobs back again, and only a small number of them came back to their original employment.

In addition to the responsibility for covering domestic work fully, there were other elements which prevented women from coming back to job fields. According to a survey, 81.8% of 35–39 year-old women answering this question and 72.4% of those above 40 said that they couldn't find jobs because of age limitations. As the research described before, because the system of most Japanese companies was to train their employees who had just finished school in order to fit the companies' needs by taking the time, they didn't accept older people. This meant that age limitations were imposed onto women when they applied for full-time job positions again. 83.9% of all companies in Japan had age limitation policies on their books with the average limitation being 37.3 years of age and the youngest limitation being 32.3 years of age. The average age that women with higher education finished taking care of their children was about 40 years old. For this reason, age limitations were big obstacles for women who wanted to reenter the job field (The Ministry of Labor in Japan, 1999). This situation did not change very much even after 2010. In the case of part-time jobs, though age limitations were usually between 40 to 49 years old and sometimes even over 50, the part-time jobs were dead-end office work which most women with four-year college degrees were not satisfied to do. This was another reason why they didn't take even part-time jobs.

The higher the education women had, the more they were interested in teaching positions than working in companies. According to *Josei Rôdô Hakusho* (1998), the most interesting jobs for women with four-year college degrees and graduate degrees were teaching positions including tutorial schools and fitness centers. Though this questioner allowed women to choose more than one answer, 97.2% of all college or graduate school women answering this survey said that they were interested in teaching positions while only 43.5% of women with junior college degrees told us so. As for working positions in companies, 17.8% of women having college and graduate degrees liked to take executive or general positions while only 11.7% of women finishing junior colleges did so. Some 34.8% of women obtaining college and graduate degrees wanted to do office work which were assistant positions helping men, while 44% of women with junior college degrees saw this work as rewarding.

Regarding women with graduate degrees, Table 34 and Table 35 shows that most of them found their jobs in special and technical fields. In 2007, 9,380 out of 13,416 (69.9%) women with masters degrees found their jobs in the special and technical fields, while 2,295 (17.1%) of them did so in office work including general positions. In the same year, 2,100 out of 2,270 (92.5%) women finishing their doctoral courses engaged in special and technical fields while only 71 (3.1%) of them obtained jobs in office work. The woman with a graduate degree was more inclined to get a job in a special or technical field, but these positions were limited and most of them were occupied by men. We can see this situation from Table 31 talking about the percentage of women engaging in occupations. The percentage of women here with graduate degrees was much lower than those of women with junior college and four-year college degrees. For example, there were many female researchers who didn't have social positions such as professors and so forth.

Tokyo Asahi Shimbun (2002, January 24) described that in universities, the position for most of the female faculty who were in their early 40s was that of assistant while 75% of male faculty who were in the same generation were associate professors. Almost half of the male faculty who were in their late 40s reached the rank of full professor and 25% of those left were associate professor. On the other hand, more than 60% of the female faculty in the same generation were assistant level and less than 20% of them had reached associate professor.

Regarding mathematics, science and engineering fields, there were very few female faculty members. For instance, in national universities, 2.65% of all the mathematics and science faculty, and 1.34% of all engineering faculty were women (Tachi, 1999, March). Even in 2010 this situation still did not improve (Takita, 2010, February 21). There were still some biases towards the female faculty and they were sometimes insulted because they were women. This may be the one of the reasons that very few members of the faculty were women.

According to Tachi (1999, March), the total number of university faculty was 144,308 and the female faculty, including assistants, was 17,782. The percentage of female faculty was 12.32% of the total, and 10.14% without including female assistants. This meant that one out of 10 on the faculty was a woman. The percentage of female faculty in national universities was 6.57% of all faculty in national universities in Japan, that in public universities was 13.97%, and in private universities was 12.23% when we ignore the number of assistants. The percentage of female presidents and vice presidents in national universities was negligible, 0.02% of all university faculty and that of female professors was 16.25% of the total staff. The percentage of female associate professors there was 25.22% and that of female full-time instructors was 12.83%; that of female assistants being 12.83%. The percentage of female presidents and vice presidents in public universities was 0.57% of all university faculty while that of female professors there was 20.31%. The percentage of female associate professors there was 21.83% and that of female full-time instructors was 18.14%; that of female assistants being 39.15%. The percentage of female presidents and vice presidents in private universities was 0.30% of all university faculty and that of female professors was 24.67%. The percentage of female associate professors there was 20.80% and that of female full time instructors was 18.9%, that of assistants being 35.30%.

Monbu Kagaku Tôkei Yôran (2011) described that the total number of university faculty was 174,403 in 2010. Of this total, the number of female faculty including assistants was 35,054. The percentage of female faculty was 20.1% of the total. The percentage of female presidents in all universities was 9.0% and that of female vice presidents was 7.2%. The percentage of female professors was 12.5% of the total staff, and that of female associate professors being 20.4%. The percentage of female full-time instructors there was 28.3% and that of female assistants was 53.5%.

All the data make it clear that higher positions were occupied by male faculty while lower positions such as assistants were for female faculty.

After World War II, women were to obtain equal opportunities in education but didn't receive equal opportunities in occupation. Actually, there were some opinions saying that although women didn't feel discrimination between genders when studying in college, they recognized it in work places. Japanese society was still male-centered and the consciousness of most of the men towards the women's social position was still more conservative than what the women felt about themselves.

CONCLUSION

Regarding the research question (How women's higher education and social position in Japan changed before and after World War II?; If their social position is still low, why has it not changed very much in spite of the large numbers of women finishing higher education?), the answers to these questions should be associated with the ideas of *ryôsaikenbo*, which still remain in people's minds although most of the people are not familiar with this term anymore. Here, this paper describes how these ideas were born, although a little of this was mentioned in the first section of chapter 1, how they related to Japanese society, and how their definitions changed before and after World War II in Japan.

During the Edo Period, women had been subordinated to the will of men in society but the procedure for keeping women that way was even more carefully continued. Education for women in Edo Japan was designed to prepare them for marriage mainly to become good wives although some women's textbooks during the Edo Period mentioned some knowledge of how to discipline their children as well. It had two types; one was education for training their minds and the other was to learn the arts. The basic policy for women's education was based on the idea of Japanese Confucianism. Its foundations were the lessons of the three obediences and four behaviors, adding to simple reading and writing, poetry, spinning and sewing, cooking, playing a music instrument, the tea ceremony and creating flower arrangements, all of this without emphasizing academic education which later, people thought, did more harm than good for women. The female being a passive object in society, she was chosen for acceptance by her husband-to-be and his family. She was controlled by them, and her personality was absorbed by them. The main point of education for training women's minds was to perfectly instill the thought that women always had to obey with sincerity in their minds and hearts, being persuaded that the woman was inferior to the man not only as a cultured human decision but as a built-in natural rule as well. It was not a successful education for women in those days if she became 'irresponsible' by thinking that she was not good enough simply because she was a woman or when she pretended to follow other people in spite of her disagreement against the idea that the woman always had to obey. It was considered a successful education when she thought that once having been born as a woman, she would voluntarily and positively complete women's ways with strong subordinating decisions, devoted to sincerity, steady faithfulness and chastity. Even then, the woman should not be stubborn in her ways but flexible and harmonious with gentle, graceful speech and actions. Education, such as the arts, helped women to be flexible and harmonious in spirit. The purpose of art education at that time was to train women to have this spiritual elegance. At the same time, education for women was not to accumulate a lot of impersonal knowledge but to encourage their strong minds to fight against such tendencies with much patience and self-control (Senjû, 1981).

Following the Meiji assumption, the Japanese government accepted the Western education system to modernize the nation. Professor David Murray, who was invited from America to be an advisor to the Ministry of Education in Japan in 1873, insisted upon the importance of women's education by discussing how mothers' education influenced that of their children and that mothers were by nature the best teachers for their children (Kubota, 1978). This Western idea meant that women could become wise mothers after receiving enough structured education in all areas. It was different from Edo Japan's idea that since women were stupid by nature, spoiling their children with too much love, they were not suitable for educating their children in a broad and general way (Koyama, 1991). It was this latter sense, the idea of wise mothers, that began to show up in modern Japanese society. Early in the Meiji Period, education for women suddenly meant Western style education emphasizing academic subjects and the same education that Japanese men received. Soon, mission schools for girls were popular among people from upper-middle and high social classes. However, because this tendency was only temporally in vogue and not familiar to the ordinary person, people began to ignore this new form of education. It took some time too for the Government to accept this new modern education for women as whole because it was so totally different from women's education in the Edo Period. For this reason, and with an economic recession in Japan at that time, the percentage of girls entering schools, even primary ones, did not increase as the Japanese government had expected. The Government then began to focus on the older type of women's education, basing it on Japanese Confucianism in the Edo Era instead of the Westernized form. From the late 1880s, it pursued education to train women to develop their own Japanese character by receiving an overall influence from the idea of Japanese ultra nationalism which was also different from that of Western countries. The idea of *ryôsaikenbo* was born out of that background.

Although women's education in the Edo Period aimed at training women only to become good wives, the Meiji Government did add to this fostering wise mothers who would contribute to the nation's development as citizens by accepting the Meiji education ideas as their aim. Here, wise mothers didn't mean mothers who had obtained new Western academic education but meant instead those mothers who were training their children to support the Japanese nation in the future based on Confucian ideas of recognizing the different roles between the different genders in society. Because men and women were different physically and psychologically by nature, their roles in society were different. Women could contribute to the country as good wives and wise mothers by taking care of their husbands, developing a good home environment and by bringing up their children well (Koyama, 1991). Here, good wives meant not only those who simply obeyed their husbands, which was expected in the Edo Era, but also those who could cover and manage domestic work well by understanding the Meiji modern idea that men were to work outside while women took responsibility for domestic work inside. These duties for women made them full citizens just as much as the men in those days when Japan was viewed as a family nation composed of the Emperor (the parent), the citizens (children) and supported by the individual families. The idea of such a relationship between the Emperor and Japanese citizens (both men and women) forced to work under the Emperor's absolute power was called Japanese nationalism, which was made up by the Meiji Government. Now women could be accepted as full citizens in the role of mothers who contributed to the nation like men. This was a development of women's social position. Before then they were not permitted to see themselves even as full-fledged human beings in the Edo Period. After the Sino-Japanese War (1894–1895), the idea of training wise mothers was reinforced because the Japanese government thought Japanese victory was based on better Japanese education. Mr. Hosokawa, president of a women's school in those days, expressed the idea that the way in which women's education developed would decide how strong that country would ultimately be (Koyama, 1991).

The idea of good Japanese wives and wise mothers became a national ideology by connecting it with Japanese nationalism, and education for training women in such a way was spread mainly through *kôtô jogakkô*. After the name of middle school for girls was changed into *kôtô jogakkô* in 1891, the Ordinance for *kôtô jogakkô* was established by the Japanese government in 1899 (Tamura, 1990). The Ministry of Education said, "A sound middle class society can't be created only by educated men. It needs the co-operation of women who are educated to become good wives and wise mothers. In *kôtô jogakkô*, Japanese women can obtain training to become good wives and wise mothers who are graceful, noble, gentle and chaste having those art skills required in middle class society" (Katayama, 1978). Its curriculum emphasized moral discipline, house-keeping, childcare, hygiene, etc. without focusing on academic education. Middle class people in those days indicated people not from aristocratic society but from ordinary society. Economically, they had no problem finding food every day. Vocationally, they were government officials, medical doctors, lawyers, and others. Although women in the middle class didn't have to work along with their husbands because of poverty, they neither engaged in public outside roles nor showed up in public with their husbands. It simply wasn't done (Sekiguchi, 1978).

Here, this work examines the content of some moral textbooks used by *kôtô jogakkô* at that time. By 1901, many moral textbooks for *kôtô jogakkô* had not been published yet but the main content of a few books emphasized morals for individuals such as honesty, kindness and simplicity and for family such as filial duty, chastity and the three obediences. Although some books discussed home economics, domestic hygiene and education to children, most of the books used still received a lot of influence from the idea of Japanese Confucianism in the Edo Era. Up until then, textbooks didn't speak of women's contribution to the nation as citizens. Between 1901 to 1911, morals for society such as charity and public hygiene and for the nation as a whole appeared in moral textbooks. Most of the books insisted on the importance of women's contribution towards not only domestic work but also the Japanese nation by clearly describing the different roles between men and women (e.g., men = outside and women = inside) based on gender differences. They also said, "Good wives should take care of their husbands with chastity, follow parents-in-law, and be nice to relatives and friends by paying attention to keeping harmony in the house. Wise mothers should train their children well with enough moral sense." Those textbooks focused on fostering good wives with women's morals rather than on being wise mothers. Although the idea of three obediences disappeared, women were still required to take second place. During this time, half of the textbooks recommended that women have some skills for outside work to earn income 'just in case', while insisting that they cover all of their domestic work perfectly (Koyama, 1981). These statements were added after the Russo-Japanese War (1904–1905) as there existed many widows because of this war (Nakanishi, 1999).

Regarding women's higher education, there were two schools, Tokyo Joshi Kôtô Shihan Gakkô and Nara Joshi Kôtô Shihan Gakkô, established by the Japanese government, as well as other famous private women's *senmongakkô* established by the Japanese for girls such as Tsuda Juku Senmongakkô, Tokyo Joi Gakkô, Joshi Bijutsu Gakkô, Nihon Joshi Daigakkô, Kyoritsu Joshi Gakuen and Jissen Joshi Gakuen. Kobe Jogakuin Senmongakkô and Tokyo Joshi Daigaku were Western style women's *senmongakkô*. The Meiji Era was indeed the dawn of women's higher education and many other women's private *senomongakkô* were established as well.

National education policies for women influenced the two national women's normal schools and women's *senmongakkô*. Tokyo Joshi Kôtô Shihan Gakkô was set up in 1874 with the new ideas motivating its curriculum. But during the late 1880s, this school's curriculum changed from centers comprising courses of intellectual content to moral discipline courses and domestic work centers based on the idea of *ryôsaikenbo* as related to nationalism. Nara Joshi Kôtô Shihan Gakkô established in 1908 perfectly followed this policy because this idea had permeated the public completely by this time. This school produced many female educators who would be good models for women who could contribute to the Japanese nation as good wives and wise mothers. In the case of Japanese private women's *senmongakkô*, most of them also were more or less influenced by this national policy and followed it closely. Kyôritsu Joshi Gakuen proudly said, "The purpose of this school is to offer students high-level technical arts, focusing on women's moral discipline and to train women who are going to become good wives and wise mothers inside and who are going to become good teachers for secondary education levels outside" (Amano, 1986). Many women's *senmongakkô* established the courses of housekeeping, sewing and home economics because among the public these courses were thought of as being useful for women who were going to manage their houses as good wives and wise mothers after their marriages. Even Western style women's *senmongakkô* was not an exception. In this new spreading atmosphere, focusing on Japanese nationalism based on the idea of the family whose center was the Emperor and the idea of Confucianism, these schools had a hard time obtaining enough students to support themselves financially as long as they insisted upon Western individualism and the idea of Christianity. Kobe Jogakuin Senmongakkô, for example, made up a school song whose words sang of the Emperor's absolute power (Kobe Jogakuin 100 nenshi Henshû Iinkai, 1982) and set up a program of home economics for the women who prepared for their marriage emphasizing moral discipline instead of an academic curriculum (Amano, 1986). It is not too much to say that women's higher education in Japan in those days more or less reinforced the educational philosophies accepted by *kôtô jogakkô*, although how much these theories were accepted depended on each school's policy and there existed individual school differences. Because the Japanese education system was (and still is) based on centralization, the Ministry of Education had strong powers to control even private schools.

After Tohoku Teikoku Daigaku's science department accepted three female students in 1913, other imperial universities and some private colleges opened their schools to female students. However, not all the schools which accepted female students as regular students would allow them to receive their Bachelor degrees. Most of the schools simply accepted them as students to audit courses or as students for special courses which didn't offer degrees. Moreover, most of them also had the added condition that female students were able to be accepted only when there were vacant seats available after male students were accepted. This condition towards female students was still unequal when compared with that of men. There were also differences among departments on which ones were to accept female students and which were not. Actually, there were still many colleges which refused to accept female students because of faculty disagreements. College education at that time was still only for the small number of women dedicated to pursuing an academic education. It was still not for ordinary people.

Once the imperial universities in Japan started accepting female students and more women began to earn secondary and higher education, the Japanese government established Rinji Kyôiku Kaigi in 1917 and reviewed Japanese education as a whole. Though both women's secondary and higher education were examined at this time, there were no big developments concerning these issues. At almost the same time, the issue as to whether male colleges should be opened to female students came under discussion and this issue led in turn to a discussion of coeducation vs. single gender education. In addition, private women's *senmongakkô* and both national *joshi kôtô shihan gakkô* began to consider raising their schools to be women's colleges. In 1940, although Kyôiku Shingikai submitted opinions about establishing women's high schools and women's colleges to the Prime Minister, they didn't materialize because of the overriding emergency situations of World War II. On March 18, 1945 the Japanese government decided to stop all education except for elementary students since the situation in Japan did not allow people to study easily.

While a number of movements relating to women's higher education did surface between 1913 and World War II, the number of female students actually engaged in higher education at imperial universities and colleges in those days remained small. According to a survey in 1941, in all of Japan, there were only eight female graduate students, 87 female regular college students and 108 other female students, including students to audit courses and special courses. The total number of these students came to only 0.42% of all students who were studying at college and graduate schools in those days. Coeducational classes were not planned. Establishing national women's *senmongakkô* and national women's colleges did not seem practical because the Japanese government's idea towards women's education was based mainly on the ideas of *ryôsaikenbo*. Since the Japanese government thought the purpose of higher education was to offer special knowledge mainly for vocations or for independent survival, it did not focus on developing women's higher education very much during this period.

Regarding occupations before World War II, from Table 2 (p.85), Table 3 (p.86), Table 5 (p.88) and Table 7 (p.90), we can discern that the total percentage of getting jobs after women finished higher education was not so high, although Tokyo Joshi Kôtô Shihan Gakkô and Nara Joshi Kôtô Shihan Gakkô had very high rates. One of the reasons why these schools had such high rates was that women finishing these schools had the duty of engaging in teaching positions for at least half of the period they learned in their schools after their graduation (Sasaki, 2002). In those days, popular jobs among women having higher education were teachers and medical workers. Even if they engaged in these jobs and worked as same as men did, their salaries were much lower than those of men. However, this situation was natural in those days when people thought that women should always be in a secondary position and help men primarily. As for women graduating from general *senmongakkô*, only one out of three obtained outside jobs. The percentages of those obtaining jobs among students graduating from Kobe Jogakuin and Tokyo Joshi Daigaku whose school policies emphasized women's financial independence based on the idea of Christianity, were only 10% and 35% respectively in 1942 (Table 7). From this data, here again the idea of *ryôsaikenbo* created by the Japanese government seems to have exerted much influence even on these women. There was, however, another reason why the number of women receiving jobs was not large. Most of the students in *senmongakkô* were from the middle and upper classes and didn't have to work to make a living. Actually, women having *senmongakkô* degrees were promised a wife's position with leaders of the Government (Amano, 1986). Japanese society needed highly educated women to match up with highly educated men. In short, higher education for women was not a step up to gain a high social position for themselves but a kind of visa allowing them to marry elite men because of the ideas of *ryôsaikenbo*.

Almost half of the women earning higher education chose institutions whose purpose was not to prepare them to get jobs but to give them a broad liberal arts education to help them become good wives and wise mothers. This was what the Meiji Government in Japan required of the women at that time and it was the common thinking of people until after World War II. These institutions chose girls from the upper or middle classes and educated them so that they could become wives of elite men. At that time, only a few women out of 1000 attended higher education and their academic career proved their status. For example, they were from the upper or middle classes, and they were smart enough because they completed their higher education. This then meant that they could become good wives and wise mothers with broad liberal arts talents and with the kind of well-bred discipline women should have.

Here again, this work explains the concepts of the ideas of *ryôsaikenbo* before World War II. It was common for Japanese women to live with their parents-in-law after their marriages if her husband was the first son, because Japanese nationalism emphasized the importance of family (Kobayashi, 1979). The woman should cover her roles as a wife, a mother and a daughter-in-law, understanding that her contributions towards the Japanese nation were in good management of her household and the raising of her children. She should also have acquired some skills to earn an income just in case of emergencies (Koyama, 1991). She should devote herself to her parents-in-law and husband and always help her husband with a faithful aid so that he could engage in his outside job without worrying about his family. She should also not only cover housekeeping, sewing, cooking, hygiene and health but also have the ability to manage the house economically. In addition, she should bring up her children well by giving them good discipline and enough education (Kobayashi, 1979). After World War I (1914–1919), the nuclear family was born as a middle class group in the center of cities. Husbands' salaries could support their families financially and a new type of housewife was born (Wasaki, 2002). In this case, the role of daughter-in-law was not expected so much, although the number of nuclear families in those days was still small. After World War I, some liberal opinions also recommended that married women have outside jobs to obtain income because of the influence from Western ideas, but this meant neither that women were allowed to engage in the same jobs as men were nor that having a job was a first priority for women. Among some people, the expression "business woman" still carried an insulting connotation. Even if she did have an outside job, she still had to take full responsibility for domestic work, taking care of her children, husband and parents-in-law by understanding the different roles between men and women (Koyama, 1991).

During World War II, the Japanese government required married women to become ideal mothers for the country, thinking much of the military. This requirement was for mothers who had sons. "The mother for a militaristic country, Japan" should think of her son not just as her own child but as her family's child and the Japanese nation's child and so encourage her son to earn reknown for himself by contributing to the country and the Emperor even if he had to die for him. When her husband and son died in the war, she never cried in public. Becoming a woman who had a soft heart and a strong mind was one of the important elements for *ryôsaikenbô* during war time (Kobayashi, 1979). During this time, the positions of good wives and wise mothers required them not only to take care of family affairs but also to nurse wounded soldiers and look after bereaved families (Wasaki, 2002).

After World War II, the Potsdam Declaration was issued on July 27, 1945 and Japan surrendered by accepting conditions to remove militarism forever, to make its territory smaller and to respect human rights by thinking of the rights of individuals as in a democracy. Based on the Potsdam Declaration, in September, 1945 General Douglas MacAthur, Supreme Commander for the Allied Powers, came to Japan to carry out the Allies' policies, recognizing the necessity for educational reform in Japan. The Japanese Emperor lost absolute power, becoming just a collective symbol for the nation as a whole. The period of Japanese nationalism was over. Education reform after World War II in Japan constituted a big change in the history of Japanese education. This reform couldn't have been achieved without the contribution of an American education mission comprised of 27 American educational specialists. Even if the Japanese people had tried to carry it out by themselves, it would either have been very difficult for them or they would have taken a long time to complete it. The framework for this reform was put in place in less than seven years by SCAP (Katayama, 1984). The biggest educational reform after World War II in Japan was the single-track 6-3-3-4 educational system introduced by America. Before World War II, there were different educational systems based on social status, but this new system very much helped ordinary people as well as women to obtain equal educational opportunities in Japan.

Regarding women's higher education, the contribution of two female experts, LuLu H. Holmes and Helen M. Hosp as advisors from America should not be overlooked. Their advice was based on their own experiences as Dean of Women at colleges in America and as members of AAUW.

They helped female students adjust to the new atmosphere of coeducation and new women's colleges, giving them counseling and guidance for their school life and finding jobs for them after their graduation (Tsuchiya, 1994). They also emphasized establishing women's associations such as JACA and set up basic issues for improving women's higher education after World War II in Japan. They made an effort not only to obtain equal educational opportunities for women but also to help female students be ready for acceptance by focusing on their importance as qualified women on the job (Uemura, 1995).

Nihonkoku Kenpô guaranteeing human rights based on democracy became a foundation to develop women's education in Japan legally. Furthermore, the idea of equal educational opportunities between men and women prescribed here were strengthened by Kyôiku Kihonhô in discussing educational ideas and principles and Gakkô Kyôikuhô in describing school systems. As for women's higher education, although equal educational opportunities between men and women based on coeducation and the establishment of women's colleges had been discussed by some radical educators and the Ministry of Education in Japan following 1868 and the Meiji Restoration, they had never come true (Murata, 1980). However, they were carried out immediately after setting up the new educational system.

After World War II, women's *senmongakkô* were promoted to junior colleges and four-year colleges and a lot of new women's higher institutions were established. The national colleges were opened to women and they began to learn in coeducating schools with equal rights. The number of female students going to higher education increased year by year. According to Table 16 (p.124), Table 17 (p.124) and Table 18 (p.125), in 1955 the total number of women going to higher education after their high school level of education was 5.0% (college, 2.4% and junior college, 2.6%) while that of male students was 15.0% (college, 13.1% and junior college, 1.9%). In 2010, this situation changed to female, 56.0% (college, 45.2% and junior college, 10.8%) and male, 57.7% (college, 56.4 % and junior college, 1.3%). The percentage of female students going to graduate school after finishing college level education changed from 1.9% in 1965 to 7.1% in 2010, while that of male students did from 4.7% in 1965 to 17.4% in 2010. In 2010, the percentage of female students within the total student body of private institutions (Table 13, p.121) living at universities (both college and graduate school) was 41.1% and 73.4%, respectively, of all students (both male and female). Regarding junior college students in 2010, 88.7% of all students were female and 94.1% of them were studying in private schools (Table 15, p.122). Women's private junior colleges very much contributed to women's higher education in Japan. As for graduate students, 30.3% of all students were women and 36.1% of them were in private universities (Table 14, p.121). From this data, we can say that most of the college students and junior college students belonged to private schools while a lot of graduate students were studying at national or public universities. When it came to popular subjects in 2010, among female college students social science was the most popular and the humanities was second. Among female junior college students, generally speaking, education was first, home economics was second and the humanities was third. Regarding female graduate students, health was first, the humanities second and social sciences third.

The post war situation of female students and their higher institutions changed when compared with that of those before World War II. Before World War II, the number of women having a college education (e.g., in Tohoku Teikoku Daigaku) was very small and they made a huge effort to improve themselves by strengthening their intention of pursuing academic education. After World War II, college education expanded from that of the privilege of a few elite to mass education for women as a whole. Having a college education now became a common thing for women from the middle and upper classes to aspire to by 1955 when Japanese high economic growth began. In the 1960s, ideas that female students might upset if not destroy the structure of the Japanese nation began to appear. Most of these women didn't have outside jobs after their graduations. Even if they engaged in outside jobs, they quit soon after. As for female graduate students, since almost four years after graduating they gave up their jobs for marriage, it was very difficult to find replacements for them. In spite of finishing their higher education, most of them didn't return anything to society as a contribution. Most of their reasons for going into higher education were to obtain general knowledge and to build up friendships rather than have a professional career as women before World War II tried to achieve. College became a place to enjoy their youth after they had finished the "examination hell" for college entry and before they had to go into adult society as full-fledged working people.

Here again, this work focuses on the ideas of *ryôsaikenbo*. How did they continue after World War II? Actually, the term itself fell into disuse after 1945 (Uno, 1993). In the 1960s when Japan began to recover from the defeat of the war, ideas that men were outside workers and women belonged inside to do homemaking came back. The Ministry of Education in Japan reformed the curriculums for elementary and middle schools by including sewing and knitting in the girls' curriculums while adding subjects to learn skills and gymnastics to the boys'. The Ministry of Education also made a homemaking course mandatory for high school girls in 1969, retaining it for girls until 1989 (Uno, 1993).

CONCLUSION

After 1964 when the system of junior colleges was made permanent, the course of home economics in private women's junior colleges became generally popular among young women. The content of the course was not so different from those offered in *kôtô jogakkô* before World War II, focusing on domestic work such as housekeeping, food (cooking) and clothes (sewing). Between the 1970s and the 1990s, the courses related to earning qualifications associated with education (e.g., teacher certification) and office work (e.g., secretarial certification) were established in many private junior colleges. This indicated that private junior colleges were training future good housewives with qualifications for outside jobs which would be helpful if they needed to work to get money. This implication was hardly different from the ideas of *ryôsaikenbo* before World War II. However, the image of *ryôsaikenbo* did change a little. In the postwar era the images of the devoted mother were stronger than the images of wife following her husband and parents-in-law. Although generally, she was still more or less required to obey these people as a good wife and daughter-in-law, her position became improved because of the new Japanese constitution's wording about the equality between men and women and because of the increase of nuclear families, especially in cities. The wife, who had the right to manage all household affairs by taking full responsibility for her children and supporting her husband who was working outside the home to obtain income for his family, was clearly contributing to the development of the Japanese country. The idea based on nationalism that women had to take care of the children who were going to contribute to the welfare of their families and the larger family of the Japanese nation under the Emperor disappeared: however, the idea of different gender's different roles still remained strong. There are still parents thinking that marriage is more important for women than studying hard to find a good job and achieve a higher social standing as a skilled human being.

In the 1990s, some schools were changed from women's schools to coed schools by establishing new departments befitting students' and social needs as a whole and by trying to change the male-oriented society ideas by casting off the philosophy of developing good wives and wise mothers.

Regarding occupations, it is getting more common for women with higher education to engage in outside jobs after just finishing their schooling. Before World War II and just after, most of the women finishing higher education obtained jobs associated with special or technical employment such as technical experts, teachers, those engaged in health and medical fields and artists. Because of the Japanese high economic growth which followed, the rate of employment for office work in enterprises increased. Job opportunities in office work were given to female students from junior colleges more than to those from four-year colleges because Japanese enterprises didn't see the need for women from four-year colleges. Women with junior college degrees took the place of women with high school degrees because the number of the former women increased and they could manage the more complicated jobs required during high economic growth. Before 1986, the purpose of office work for women was to help men as assistants, and these were dead-end jobs. Even if women with four-year college degrees obtained office work, they were not given the same jobs as men and their conditions were not so different from that of women with junior college degrees. It was also impossible for them to accumulate career advantages. This condition began to change when the Japanese government established the Ordinance of Equal Opportunities in Occupation act between men and women in 1986. Women with four-year college degrees were allowed to win the same jobs as four-year college men, and so make it possible for women to obtain even executive positions. However, this ordinance didn't actually work out well enough to help women's job positions become better. Although the ordinance spoke of equality in occupations between men and women as established, it still seemed to take time for people to accept it. Old rules that women's positions should be as assistants for men persisted and the expectation that women should quit their jobs after their marriage and deliveries remained in people's consciousness. A big problem was that most people (both men and women) still thought that women needed to take full responsibility for domestic work plus taking care of their children and old sick parents, even if they had full-time outside jobs. Due to this, there are still many women quitting their jobs after marriage and having babies, although some of them are back after they finish taking care of their children. Since women need to pile up recognizable credits in their career with a company for a long time to obtain an executive position, the number of female executives in enterprises is small. As for the academic world such as colleges and universities in general, the number of female professors is also small and most of them are assistant and associate professors, assisting male professors. It is still a male-centered society. From these results, the ideas of *ryôsaikenbo* born a long time ago still exert influence over the occupational world in Japan.

Ryôsaikenbo was women's ideal social position based on the male point of view adjusting to the needs of changing times. The meanings of *ryôsaikenbo* itself changed—good wives in the Edo Era, wise mothers just after the Meiji Restoration and good wives and wise mothers following the Russo-Japanese War. After World War I, the element of having an outside job which didn't interrupt required domestic work was added and that of mother for Japan's militaristic state was required during World War II. Although such roles as wives and mothers were expected of women from way back in our history, they were actually created as a national policy by the Japanese government (Koyama, 1995).

After World War II, equal opportunities in education and coeducation were permitted in laws, the system of mass education was spread and a lot of female students came to obtain higher education. Although now they enjoy college lives without the pressure of inferiority which earlier women had to face while finding various jobs in society, the percentage of those continuing in their jobs is still low. Higher education has spread but it seems not to have contributed very much towards helping women to be independent both economically and mentally, nor has it changed completely the traditional view that women should still take full responsibility for domestic work, taking care of their children and old sick parents by understanding the different gender's different roles. The Ordinance of Equal Opportunities in Occupation act between men and women, established in 1986, made it possible for women with four-year college degrees to be given the same jobs as men in companies. However, the number of women engaging in outside jobs as men do still remains small, because it is very difficult, almost impossible, for women to cover both domestic work and full-time outside jobs perfectly even though they may want to work as hard as men do for the same results. The present situation requires women to work twice as hard as men do. For this reason, in general, even if women have outside jobs, they can have, at most, part-time jobs, most of which will not lead to promotion, nor realize enough in salary to support a family well in spite of her raised qualifications and expectations. Because of this, women need to depend on men financially, which keeps women in a secondary role in society even now. As long as domestic work remains unpaid, in spite of women's hard work, men's positions remain superior to that of women economically. Regarding universities and colleges, it is still difficult for women to become professors and there are many researchers who don't have social positions such as professors but are just assistants probably because of the traditional idea that women should be in the secondary position. Some of them (both men and women) are still apt to deny even the idea that women have outside jobs because of the idea of different genders' different roles. A woman with a full-time outside job said, "I'm a bad wife because I can't cover domestic work including looking after my children well. I should quit my job." However, there is no man who admits to being a bad husband if he doesn't participate in domestic work in Japan. Although women successfully won equal situations in education after World War II, they are still struggling to obtain equal situations in occupations and in social position. It is difficult to forget the ideas of *ryôsaikenbo* which have indeed permeated deep into people's minds, even though this term has been dead for a long time already.

References

Abe Yoshio (1965). *Nichibei no shushigaku to Chôsen.* Tokyo: Tokyo Daigaku Shuppankai.
Abe Yoshio (1974). Nihon no shushigaku. *Shushigaku nyûmon,* 137–158.
Akatsuka Tomoko (2000). Sôritsusya Naruse Jinzô no kyôiku rinen to kasei gakubu. *Nihon Joshi Daigaku Sôgô Kenkyûsho Nyûsu,* 9, 10–14.
Amano Masako (1978). Daiichiji taisengo ni okeru joshi kôtô kyôiku no shakaiteki kinô. *Kyôiku Shakaigaku Kenkyû,* 33, 118–131.
Amano Masako (Ed.) (1986). *Joshi kôtô kyôiku no zahyô.* Tokyo: Kakiuchi Shuppan Kabushiki Gaisha.
Aoki Seiko (1981). *Nihon joshidai no 80 nen.* Tokyo: Tosho Insatsu Kabushiki Gaisha.
Aoki Seiko (1995). Joshi daigaku no gendaiteki igi. In Nihon Joshi Daigaku Joshi Kyôiku Kenkyûsho (Eds.), *Joshi daigakuron* (pp.10–25). Tokyo: Domesu Shuppan.
Aoyanagi Seiichi (1992, June 15). Meijiki no kaigyôi to igaku kyôiku. *Nihon Ishikai Zasshi,* 107, (12), 2221–2223.
Bandô Reiko (2011, July 27). Josei no shakai sanka. *The Yomiuri Shimbun.*
Bungei Shunjû (1965, September). Ganbare! joshidaisei, 178–184.
Burke Peter (1991). *New perspectives on historical writing.* New York: Penn State Press.
Chino Yôichi (1989). *Kindai nihon fujin kyôikushi.* Tokyo: Domesu Shuppan.
Chûô Shokugyô Shôkai Jimukyoku (1927). *Shôwa ninen sangatsu sotsugyô zenkoku daigaku senmongakkôsei shûshoku jôkyô chôsa.* Tokyo: F. Mamiya & Co.
Chûô Shokugyô Shôkai Jimukyoku (1935). *Chishiki kaikyû shûshoku ni kansuru shiryô.* Tokyo: Gômei Gaisha Fuji Insatsusha.
Chûô Shokugyô Shôkai Jimukyoku (1937). *Shôwa 11 nendo chishiki kaikyû shûshoku ni kansuru shiryô.* Tokyo: Kabushiki Gaisha Isseisha.
Dôshisha Shashi Shiryô Henshûsho (1965). *Dôshisha 90 nen shoshi.* Kyoto: Nihon Shashin Insatsu Kabushiki Gaisha.
Fairbank, John King (1973). *East Asia:tradition and trasformation.* Boston: Houghton Miffli.
Fujii, Harue (1973). *Nihon no joshi kôtô kyôiku.* Tokyo: Domesu Shuppan.
Fujin Kôron (1957, December). Joshi daigakusei ni tozasareta doa, 316–326.
Fujo Shimbun (1919, March 14). Joshi sôgô daigaku no naiyô. No. 982.
Fujo Shimbun (1919, May 23). Danshi daigaku kaihô mondai. No.992.
Fujo Shimbun (1919, November 30). Joshi kôtô kyôiku no seigan. No.1019.
Fujo Shimbun (1920, January 18). Keidai sôdai no joshi nyûgaku fukyoka. No. 1026.
Fujo Shimbun (1920, September 19). Teidai bungakubu zenkaihô. No. 1061.
Fukaya Masashi (1981). *Ryôsaikenbo shugi no kyôiku.* Tokyo: Reimeishobô.
Fukushima Shirô (1920, April 4). Danjo kyôgaku mondai, jô. *Fujo Shimbun.* No. 1037.
Gunjishima Hiromi & Takaguchi Yasuyuki (1992). Nara joshi kôtô shihan gakkô no jûseikatsu kyôiku. *Kaseigaku Kenkyû,* 38, (2), 109–115.
Handa Tatsuko (1986). Kasei gakubu. In M., Amano (Ed.), *Joshi kôtô kyôiku no zahyô*

(pp.95-118). Tokyo: Kakiuchi Shuppan Kabushiki Gaisha.

Harrington Ann (1987). Women and higher education in the Japanese Empire (1895-1945). *Journal of Asian History*, 21, (2), 169-186.

Hashimoto Noriko (1976). Senzen Nihon no joshi no kôtô kyôiku yôkyû to seido kôsô. *Kyôikugaku Kenkyû*, 43, (3), 12-22.

Hashimoto Noriko (1977). Fujin kenkyûsha no chii wa naze hikuika. *Rekishi Hyôron*, 94-110.

Hashimoto Noriko (1992). *Danjo kyôgaku no shiteki kenkyû*. Tokyo: Ôtsuki Shoten.

Hatanaka Rie (1999). Keihanshin ni okeru joshi kôtô kyôiku no seiritsu jijô. *Nihon Kyôiku Gakkai Nenpô*, 6, 139-154.

Hayashi K., Kobayashi S., Fukuda E., Ogawa K., Andô R., & Uchida M. (2001). Wayô Joshi Daigaku Tanki Daigaku bu no genjô to kadai. *Wayô Joshi Daigaku Kiyô*, 3, 93-115.

Hirano Seisuke (1977). *Shimbun shûsei Taishô hen nenshi hichinendo gekan*. Tokyo: Hirakawa Kôgyôsha.

Hirano Seisuke (1978). *Shimbun shûsei Taishô hen nenshi Taishô gannendoban*. Tokyo: Hirakawa Kôgyôsha.

Hirano Seisuke (1983). *Shimbun shûsei Taishô hen nenshi kunendo gekan*. Tokyo: Hirakawa Kôgyôsha.

Hirasawa Kazushi (1991). Tandai shingaku to shokugyô sentaku. *Soshioroji*, 36, (2), 87-103.

Hisaki Y. & Mita S. (1981). Jûkyûseiki zenhan Edo kinkô nôson ni okeru joshi kyôiku no ichikenkyû: Bushû Namamugi mura Sekiguchi nikki kara. *Yokohama Kokuritsu Daigaku Kyôiku Kiyô*, 21, 67-94.

Hokkaido Daigaku (1980). *Hokudai 100 nenshi bukyokushi*. Sapporo: Kabushiki Gaisha Gyôsei.

Holmes LuLu (1948). Women in the new Japan. *Journal of the American Association of University Women*, 41 (3), 137-141.

Ienega Saburô (1977). *Shin nihonshi*. Tokyo: Sanseidô.

Igasaki A. & Yoshihara K. (1975). *Beikoku kyôiku shisetsudan hôkokusho: sengo kyôiku no genten 2*. Tokyo: Shintô Insatsu Kabushuki Gaisha.

Ikeda Satoshi (1966). *Joshi daigaku*. Tokyo: Nihon Keizai Shimbun.

Ikeda Yasaburô (1962, April). Daigaku jokaron. *Fujin Kôron*, 46-48.

Ishii Runa (2000). Sengo Nihon no joshi kôtô kyôiku kaikaku ni okeru josei rîdâ no yakuwari. *Kokusai Gaku Rebyû*, 12, 67-83.

Itô Megumi (1990). CI&E kyôikuka no fujin kyôiku seisaku. In M. Ogawa & H. Shinkai (Eds.). *GHQ no shakai kyôiku seisaku seiritsu to tenkai*, (pp.209-233). Tokyo: Ôzorasha.

Japan Rinji Kyôiku Kaigi (1979a). *Rinji kyôiku kaigi dai isshû shiryô*. Tokyo: Monbushô.

Japan Rinji Kyôiku Kaigi (1979b). *Rinji kyôiku kaigi dai goshû sôkai sokkiroku dai 23-30 gô*. Tokyo: Monbushô.

Jissen Joshi Gakuen 80 nenshi Henshû Iinkai (1971). *Jissen Joshi Gakuen 80 nenshi*. Tokyo: Ôkawahara Insatsu Kabushiki Gaisha.

Josei Jishin (1966, July 25). Kutabare hanayome shugyô ni daigaku e kayou joseitachi, pp.65-69.

Joshi Bijutsu Daigaku (1980). *Joshi Bijutsu Daigaku 80 nenshi*. Tokyo: Gyôsei.

Kageyama Noboru (2000a). Sawayanagi Masatarô to joshi kôtô kyôiku. *Seijô Bungei,* 170, 48–116.
Kageyama Noboru (2000b). Taishôki rinji kyôiku gikai joshi kyôiku shingi, tôshin to Yosano Akiko no joshi kyôikuron. *Seijô Bungei,* 60–76.
Kageyama Reiko (1994). *Naruse Jinzô no kyôiku shisô.* Tokyo: Kazamashobô.
Kaigo Tokiomi (1960). *Rnji kyôiku kaigi no kenkyû.* Tokyo: Tokyo Daigaku Shuppankai.
Kameda Atsuko (1986). Joshi tanki daigaku. In M., Amano (Eds.), *Joshi kôtô kyôiku no zahyô* (pp.119–139). Tokyo: Kakiuchi Shuppan Kabushiki Gaisha.
Kaneko Motohisa (1995). *Kinmirai no daigakuzô, gendai no kôtô kyôiku san.* Tokyo: Tosho Insatsu.
Kaneshige Munekazu (1979). Meiji chûki no joshi kyôiku ni tsuite. *Tokuyama Daigaku Ronshû,* 13, 75–90.
Karasawa Tomitarô (1978). *Nihon kyôikushi.* Tokyo: Seibundô Shinkôsha.
Katayama Seiichi (1978). Ryôsaikenbo shugi kyôiku no igi. *Joshi Kyôiku,* 1, 9–16.
Katayama Seiichi (1984). *Kindai Nihon no joshi kyôiku.* Tokyo: Kenpakusha.
Keiôgijuku (1968). *Keiôgijuku 100 nenshi gekan.* Tokyo: Keiô Tsûshin Kabushiki Gaisha.
Kobayashi Sumie (1951). *Kyôiku hyakka jiten.* Tokyo: Fukumura Shoten.
Kobayashi Teruyuki (1979). Shôwa senzenki no katei kyôiku no ichi sokumen. *Shin-Shû Daigaku Kyôiku Gakubu Kiyô,* 41, 1–10.
Kobe Jogakuin 80 nenshi Henshû Iinkai (1955). *Kobe Jogakuin 80 nenshi.* Osaka: Toyo Shigyô Kabushiki Gaisha.
Kobe Jogakuin 100 nenshi Henshû Iinkai (1977). *Kobe Jogakuin 100 nenshi, sôsetsu.* Kyoto: Kahoku Insatsu Kabushiki Gaisha.
Kobe Jogakuin 100 nenshi Henshû Iinkai (1982). *Kobe Jogakuin 100 nenshi, kakuron.* Osaka: Toyo Shigyô Kabushiki Gaisha.
Koizumi Ikuko (1933). *Asuno josei kyôiku.* Tokyo: Nankôsha.
Koyama Shizuko (1981). Kôtô jogakkô kyôiku to ryôsaikenbo kan. *Kyoto Daigaku Kyôiku Gakubu Kiyô,* 3, 94–104.
Koyama Shizuko (1991). *Ryôsaikenbo to yû kihan.* Tokyo: Kabushiki Gaisha Keisô Shobô.
Koyama Shizuko (1995). Daisan teian ryôsaikenbo shisô kenkyû no tachiba kara. *Nihon no Kyôiku Shigaku,* 38, 345–349.
Kubota Yoshihiro (1978). Ryôsaikenbo kyôiku shisô no keisei to sono yakuwari. *Nihon Daigaku Jinmon Kagaku Kenkyûsho Kenkyû Kiyô,* 20, 17–31.
Kyoto Daigaku 100 nenshi Henshû Iinkai (1998). *Kyoto Daigaku 100 nenshi sôsetsuhen.* Kyoto: Kyoto Daigaku Kôenkai Heisei 10.
Kyushu Daigaku Sôritsu 50 shûnen Kinenkai (1967). *Kyushu Daigaku 50 nenshi tsûshi.* Fukuoka: Dainihon Insatsu Kabushiki Gaisha.
LY Shang Bo (1998). Josei no kôtô kyôiku to shakai sanka. *Nihon Kokusai Kyôiku Gakkai,* 4, 72–85.
Mabashi Michiko (1995). Nihon Joshi Daigaku no genjô to kadai. In Nihon Joshi Daigaku Joshi Kyôiku Kenkyûsho (Ed), *Joshi daigakuron* (pp.144–172). Tokyo: Domesu Shuppan.
MacArthur Douglas (1964). *Reminiscences.* New York: McGraw-Hill Book Company.
Makiishi Takiko (2000). Meiji Taishô no joshi kôtô kikan ni okeru shakai kyôiku.

Sendai Shirayuri Joshi Daigaku Kiyô, 11–23.
Matsumura Naoko (1984). Gendai no joshi kôtô kyôiku no ichi sokumen. *Tetsugakuronshû*, 31, 36–49.
Matsusawa Kazuko (2000). Ima naze joshi daigaku ka. In Heian Jogakuin Daigaku (Ed.), *Joshi kôtô kyôiku no atarashii yakuwari* (pp.18–27). Otsu: Sangaku Shuppan Yûgen Gaisha.
McDowell W. H. (2002). Historical research. London: Pearson Education Limited.
Minami, Hiroshi (1959, March). Sotsugyôsei wa joshidai o kô miru. *Fujin Kôron*, 108 –114.
Mizuno Machiko (1982). Jogaku Zasshi ni okeru joshi kôtô kyôikuron. *Kyôikugaku Kenkyû* 49 (3), 54–63.
Mochizuki Yosaburô (1892). *Kazokushugi joshi kyôiku*. Osaka, Fukuinsha.
Mori Masumi (1991a). Kasei kara seikatsu e. *Nihon Kasei Gakkaishi*, 42, (2), 87–91.
Môri Sachiko (1999, April). Joshi gakusei no kôgakurekika to shûshoku mondai no genzai. *Tanki Daigaku Kyôiku*, 20–27.
Mori Takao (1991b). *Gakkô shôroppô*. Tokyo: Kyodo Shuppan.
Morita Misa (2000). Sôgôshoku josei no shûgyô to katei no ryôritsu ni tsuite. *Kaseigaku Kenkyû*, 47 (1), 35–40.
Murakami Sachiko (1959, February 8). Joshidai wa hanayome gakkô ka. *Shûkan Asahi*, 30–33.
Murata Suzuko (1980). *Waga kuni joshi kôtô kyôiku seiritsu katei no kenkyû*. Tokyo: Kazamashobô.
Nagai Shinichi (2000). Joshi Bijutsu Daigaku 100 nen no ayumi. *Gekkan Bijutsu*, 26 (10), 41–47.
Nagano Midori (1988). Kajika saihôka ni miru joshi kyôiku: Meiji kara Shôwa shoki ni kakete. *Tsukuba Shakaika Kenkyû*, 7, 42–52.
Naito Yosaburô (1998). *Gakkô kyôikuhô kaisetsu*. Tokyo: Nihon Tosho Sentâ.
Nakajima Tarô (1970). *Sengo Nihon kyôiku seidô seiritsushi*. Tokyo: Iwasakigaku Shuppansha.
Nakanishi Naoki (1999). Meiji kôki ni okeru taiseiteki ryôsaikenbo shisô kakuritsu no katei. *Kenkyû Kiyô*, 12, 51–92.
Nakano Setsuko (1994). Mô hitotsu no Edo ki joshi kyôiku. *Kanazawa Daigaku Daigaku Kyôiku Kaihô Sentâ Kiyô*, 14, 59–66.
Naki Shimoda Kôchôsensei Denki Henshûsho (1989). *Shimoda Utako senseiden*. Tokyo: Ôzorasya.
Nara Joshi Daigaku 60 nenshi Henshû Iinkai (1970). *Nara Joshi Daigaku 60 nenshi*. Tokyo: Daiichi Hôki Shuppan Kabushiki Gaisha.
Nihon Ishikai Zasshi (1992). Meijiki no kaigyôi to igaku kyôiku sono kyû, 107, (12), 2221–2223.
Nihon Joshi Daigaku Kyôiku Kenkyûsho (1975). *Taishô no joshi kyôiku*. Tokyo: Kokudosha.
Nihon Joshi Daigaku Kyôiku Kenkyûsho (1987). *Joshi no kôtô kyôiku*. Tokyo: Kabushikigaisha Gyôsei.
Nihon Rikurûto Sentâ Kikaku Chôsashitsu Chôsaka (1980). *Rikurûto chôsa sôran shinki gakusotsu rôdô shijôhen*. Tokyo: Rikurûto Sentâ.
Nishi Toshio (1983). *Makkâsâ no hanzai ge*. Tokyo: Nihon Kôgyô Shimbunsha.
Oba Minako (1990). *Tsuda Umeko*. Tokyo: Asahi Shimbunsha.

Ochanomizu Joshi Daigaku 100 nenshi Kankô Iinkai (1984). *Ochanomizu Joshi Daigaku 100 nenshi*. Toky: Ochanomizu Joshi Daigaku 100 nenshi Kankô Iinkai.
Ogawa Sasuo (1967, May 7). Joshi ichi gakka o dokusensu. *Asahi Jânaru*, 50-62.
Ôishi M., Mori C., Satô S., Kawamura M., & Yamamoto S. (2000). Kaseikei daigaku ni okeru shikaku shûtoku shien no genjô to kanôsei ni kansuru ichi hôkoku. *Kamakura Joshi Daigaku Kiyô*, 7, 149-156.
Okada Noriko (1999). Sengo ni okeru joshi kôtô kyôiku kikan no kyôgakuka. *Chûgoku Shikoku Kyôiku Gakkai Kyôikugaku Kenkyû Kiyô*, 45 (1), 122-127.
Osaka Asahi Shimbun (1999, May 24). Joshi gakusei "kigyô no honne wa?" Kaisei Koyô Kintôhô 'koyô kiki'.
Ôtani Yasuko (1993). Nara jokôshi ikkisei. *Nara Joshi Daigaku Shigakukai*, 41-60.
Rodon Donald (1983). From 'old miss' to new professional: A portrait of women educators under the American occupation of Japan, 1945-52. *History of Education Quarterly*, winter, 469-490.
Rose Cynthia (Ed.). (1977). *American decades primary sources 1900-1909*. MI: Gale.
Ryôsawa Umeko (1981). Taishôki ni okeru Joshi kôtô kyôiku to shokugyô. *Kasei Keizaigaku Ronshû*, 17 (4), 75-88.
Saitô Atsuyoshi (1986). Edo jidai no katei kyôiku: Joshi no shitsuke nitsuite. *Nihon Shigaku Kyôiku Kenkyûsho Kiyô*, 21 (1), 349-380.
Sakurai Mamoru (1943). *Joshi kyôikushi*. Osaka: Zôshindô.
Sasaki Keiko (2002). *Senzenki joshi kôtô kyôiku no ryôteki kakudai katei*. Tokyo; Tokyo Daigaku Shuppankai.
Satô Yoshikazu (1999). Joshi kôtô bijutsu kyôiku no senkusha Yokoi Tamako kenkyû, ichi. *Joshi Bijutsu Daigaku Kiyô*, 29, 91-108.
Sawayanagi Masatarô (1919, March 14). Danshi no gakkô o kaihô seyo. *Fujo Shimbun*, No.982.
Sawayanagi Masatarô. Joshi kyôiku ni kansuru an. *Sawayanagi Masatarô Shika Bunsho*, 153-035, 153-036, 153-037.
Seijô Gakuen Sawayanagi Masatarô Zenshû Kankôkaihen (1980). *Sawayanagi Masatarô zenshû dai 10 kan*. Tokyo: Kokudosha.
Sekiguchi Fusa (1980). Joshi kyôiku ni okeru saihô no kyôikushiteki kenkyû: Edo Meiji ryôjidai ni okeru saihô kyôiku o chûshintoshite. *Kaseigaku Zasshi*, 31 (10), 46-55.
Sekiguchi Reiko (1978). Kenboryôsai kara ryôsaikenbo e. *Seitoku Gakuen Gifu Kyôiku Daigaku Kiyô*, 5, 81-93.
Senjû Katsumi (1981). Edo jidai no joshi kyôiku. *Kyôiku to Igaku*, 29 (1), 54-61.
Shibayama Tadashi (1993). Tanki daigaku ni okeru hisho kyôiku ni tsuite. *Nagoya Joshi Daigaku Kiyô*, 39, 99-111.
Shibukawa Hisako (1970). *Kindai nihon joseishi ichi kyôiku*. Tokyo: Kagoshima Kenkyûsho Shuppankai.
Shiga Tadashi (1977). *Nihon joshi kyôikushi*. Tokyo: Biwakoshobô.
Shimizu Masao (1994). Edo jidai ni okeru josei no gakushû. *Mejiro Gakuen Joshi Kyôiku Kenkyûsho Shohô*, 48-52.
Suzuki Eiichi (1983). *Nihon senryô to kyôiku kaikaku*. Tokyo: Keisô Shobô.
Suzuki E. & Hirahara H. (1998). *Shiryô kyôiku kihonhô 50 nenshi*. Tokyo: Keisô Shobâ.
Suzuki Isao (1999). *Chikujô gakkô kyôikuhô*. Tokyo: Gakuyô Shobô.
Suzuki Yûko (1994). *Senkushatachi no shôzô-Asu o hiraita jôseitachi*. Tokyo: Domesu

Shuppan.
Tachi Kaoru (1978). Tokyo Joshi Kôtô Shihan Gakkô no daigaku shôkaku undô. *Ochanomizu Joshi Daigaku Jinmon Kagaku Kiyô*, 59–78.
Tachi Kaoru (1999, March). Jendâ tôkei kara mita daigaku no genjô. *Josei Gaku Kenkyû* 7, 2–17.
Tago Kazutomi (1919, April 4). Joshi kôtô kyôiku no hitsuyô. *Fujo Shimbun,* No.985.
Taishô Shôwa Shimbun Kenkyûkai (1966). *Shinbum shûsei Taishô hen nenshi Taishô ninendoban.* Tokyo: Kokushô Insatsu Kabushiki Gaisha.
Takahara Sumiko (1964, September). Shimedasareta joshi daigaku sotsugyôsei. *Fujin Kôron,* 66–73.
Takahashi Tsugiyoshi (1983). Taishô Shôwa shoki ni okeru joshi kôtô kyôikushi kenkyû. *Nihon Kyôikushi no Ronkyû,* 161–183.
Takahashi Tsugiyoshi (1989). Shôwa shoki gakusei kaikaku shoan no joshi kôtô kyôiku seido kôsô ni kansuru kisoteki kenkyû. *Ajia no Kyôiku to Bunka,* 423–437.
Takase Shôtaro (1956). *Kyôritsu Joshi Gakuen 70 nenshi.* Tokyo: Kyôritsu Joshi Gakuen.
Takita Kyôko (2010, February, 21). Josei kenkyûsha saiyôritsu nobizu. *The Yomiuri Shimbun.*
Tamura Eiichirô (1990). Ryôsaikenbo shugi kyôiku no keisei to henkan. *Musashino Daigaku Jinmon Gakkai Zasshi,* 21, (3), (4), 15–32.
Tanaka Y., & Nishimura Y. (1986). Shûshoku keizoku ni oyobosu gakureki kôka. In M. Amano (Ed.) *Joshi kôtô kyôiku no zahyô,* (pp.203–224). Tokyo: Kakiuchi Shuppan Kabushiki Gaisha.
Tanioka Ikuko (1997). Kindai Nihon joshi kôtô kyôiku no seiritsu to sono kihon dezain. *Chûkyo Daigaku Kiyô,* 79–111.
Tanioka Ikuko (2000). Nihon ni okeru joshi kôtô kyôiku no 100 nen. *Kyôiku to Jôho,* 8 –13.
Terasawa Miyoko (1991). Kobe Jogakuin ni okeru jinrui yûai no seishin to kokusai kôryu no suishin. *Nihon Eigo Kyôikushi Kenkyû,* 7, 183–196.
Teruoka Yasutaka (1962, March). Joshi gakusei yo ni habakaru. *Fujin Kôron,* 277–281.
Teruoka Yasutaka (1962, June 29). Joshi gakusei wa bôkoku ka kôkoku ka. *Shûkan Asahi,* 12–13.
The Cabinet Office in Japan (2009, February). *Kyôdô Sankaku.* Retrived March 19, 2009 from http://www.gender.go.jp/main_contents/category/kyodo/200902/200902-05.html
The Gender Equality Bureau Cabinet Office (2011, January). *Kyôdô Sankaku.* Retrived March 25, 2012 from mhtml:file://C:\Documents and Settings\Administrator\デスクトップ\「共同参画」2011…
The Minisrty of Education, Culture, Sports, Scienece, and Technology in Japan (2006). *Gakkô Kihon Chôsa Hôkokusho.* Tokyo: Kokuritsu Insatsu Kyoku.
The Minisrty of Education, Culture, Sports, Science, and technology in Japan (2011). *Gakkô Kihon Chôsa Hôkokusho.* Tokyo: Kokuritsu Insatsu Kyoku.
The Ministry of Education, Culture, Sports, Science, and Techonology in Japan (2006). *Monbu Kagaku Tôkei Yôran.* Tokyo: Kokuritsu Insatsu Kyoku.
The Ministry of Education, Culture, Sports, Science, and Techonology (2011). *Monbu Kagaku Tôkei Yôran.* Tokyo: Kokuritsu Insatsu Kyoku.

The Ministry of Education in Japan (1956). *Gakkô Kihon Chôsa Hôkokusho*. Tokyo: Ôkura Insatsu Kyoku.
The Ministry of Education in Japan (1959). *Gakkô Kihon Chôsa Hôkokusho*. Tokyo: Ôkura Insatsu Kyoku.
The Ministry of Education in Japan (1961). *Gakkô Kihon Chôsa Hôkokusho*. Tokyo: Ôkura Insatsu Kyoku.
The Ministry of Education in Japan (1966). *Gakkô Kihon Chôsa Hôkokusho*. Tokyo: Ôkura Insatsu Kyoku.
The Ministry of Education in Japan (1971). *Gakkô Kihon Chôsa Hôkokusho*. Tokyo: Ôkura Insatsu Kyoku.
The Ministry of Education in Japan (1976). *Gakkô Kihon Chôsa Hôkokusho*. Tokyo: Ôkura Insatsu Kyoku.
The Ministry of Education in Japan (1981). *Gakkô Kihon Chôsa Hôkokusho*. Tokyo: Ôkura Insatsu Kyoku.
The Ministry of Education in Japan (1986). *Gakkô Kihon Chôsa Hôkokusho*. Tokyo: Ôkura Insatsu Kyoku.
The Ministry of Education in Japan (1991). *Gakkô Kihon Chôsa Hôkokusho*. Tokyo: Ôkura Insatsu Kyoku.
The Ministry of Education in Japan (1996a). *Gakkô Kihon Chôsa Hôkokusho*. Tokyo: Ôkura Insatsu Kyoku.
The Ministry of Education in Japan (2000). *Gakkô Kihon Chôsa Hôkokusho*. Tokyo: Ôkura Insatsu Kyoku.
The Minisrty of Education in Japan (2001). *Gakkô Kihon Chôsa Hôkokusho*. Tokyo: Ôkura Insatsu Kyoku.
The Ministry of Education in Japan (1923). *Monbushô Nenpô 48*. Gifu: Nishino Insatsu Kabushiki Gaisha Shiten.
The Ministry of Education in Japan (1936). *Monbushô Nenpô 58*. Tokyo: Tôa Insatsu Kabushiki Gaisha.
The Ministry of Education in Japan (1970). *Monbushô Nenpô 38*. Tokyo: Yûgen Gaisha Senbundô.
The Ministry of Education in Japan (1979). *Monbushô Nenpô 68*. Tokyo: Bunsendô Shuppan Kabushiki Gaisha.
The Ministry of Education in Japan (1942). *Monbushô Nenpô 70*. Tokyo: Daiichi Hôki Shuppan.
The Ministry of Education in Japan (1956). *Monbu Tôkei Yôran*. Tokyo: Daiichi Hôki Shuppan.
The Ministry of Education in Japan (1959). *Monbu Tôkei Yôran*. Tokyo: Daiichi Hôki Shuppan.
The Ministry of Education in Japan (1966). *Monbu Tôkei Yôran*. Tokyo: Daiichi Hôki Shuppan.
The Ministry of Education in Japan (1976). *Monbu Tôkei Yôran*. Tokyo: Daiichi Shuppan.
The Ministry of Education in Japan (1981). *Monbu Tôkei Yôran*. Tokyo: Daiichi Shuppan.
The Ministry of Education in Japan (1986). *Monbu Tôkei Yôran*. Tokyo: Daiichi Shuppan.
The Ministry of Education in Japan (1991). *Monbu Tôkei Yôran*. Tokyo: Daiichi Shup-

pan.
The Ministry of Education in Japan (1996b). *Monbu Tôkei Yôran*. Tokyo: Daiichi Shuppan.
The Ministry of Education in Japan (2001). *Monbu Tôkei Yôran*. Tokyo: Daiichi Shuppan.
The Ministry of Labor, Health, and Warefare in Japan (2007). *Josei Koyô Kanri Kihon Chôsa Hôkokusho*. Tokyo: Kôsei Rôdôshô Koyô Kintô, Jidô Katei Kyoku Koyô Kintô Seisakuka.
The Ministry of Labor, Health, and Welfare in Japan (2009). *Josei rôdô no bunseki 2008 nen*. Tokyo: Zaidan Hôjin 21 Seiki Shokugyô Zaidan.
The Ministry of Labor in Japan (1995). *Josei Rôdô Hakusho*. Tokyo: 21 Seiki Shokugyô Zaidan.
The Ministry of Labor in Japan (1998). *Josei Rôdô Hakusho*. Tokyo: 21 Seiki Shokugyô Zaidan.
The Ministry of Labor in Japan (1999). *Josei Rôdô Hakusho*. Tokyo: 21 Seiki Shokugyô Zaidan.
The Ministry of Labor in Japan (2000). *Josei Rôdô Hakusho*. Tokyo: 21 Seiki Shokugyô Zaidan..
The Ministry of Welfare & Labor in Japan (1998). *Josei Koyô Kanri Kihon Chôsa Hôkokusho*. Tokyo: Rôdôshô Josei Kyoku.
The Yomiuri Shimbun (1995, November, 7). Kawaru shokuba ugoku koyô, dai nibu kikai kintô (1) kieyuku jimushoku.
The Yomiuri Shimbun (2008, November 14). Josei sabetsu kaizen nihon ni kankoku.
Tohoku Daigaku (1960). *Tohoku Daigaku 50 nenshi*. Sendai: Ôtotsuban Insatsu Kabushiki Gaisha.
Tokyo Asahi Shimbun (1913, August 16). Sanjoshi daigaku ni Hairu.
Tokyo Asahi Shimbun (1913, August 22). Joshi to gakushigô.
Tokyo Asahi Shimbun (2002, January 24). Joshi kenkyûsha shôshin ni kabe.
Tokyo Daigaku 100 nenshi Iinkai (1984). *Tokyo Daigaku 100 nenshi tsûshi*. Tokyo: Tokyo Daigaku Shuppankai.
Tokyo Daigaku 100 nenshi Iinkai (1989). *Tokyo Daigaku 100 nenshi bukyokushi*. Tokyo: Daiichi Hôki Shuppan Kabushiki Gaisha.
Tokyo Joshi Daigaku 80 nenshi Henshû Iinkai (1998). *Tokyo Joshi Daigaku no 80 nen*. Tokyo: Egadô Shuppan Kabushiki Gaisha.
Tokyo Joshi Ika Daigaku (1966). *Tokyo Joshi Ika Daigaku shôshi*. Tokyo: Chûôkôron Jigyô Shuppan.
Tokyo Joshi Kôtô Shihan Gakkô Henshû (1934). *Tokyo Joshi Kôtô Shihan Gakkô 60 nenshi*. Tokyo: Tokyo Joshi Kôtô Shihan Gakkô.
Tokyo Joshi Shûshoku Shidôkai (1994). *Onna to shokugyô Tokyo joshi shûshoku annai*. Tokyo: Ôzorasha.
Tokyo Teikoku Daigaku (1932). *Tokyo Teikoku Daigaku 50 nenshi*. Tokyo: Chûgai Insatsu Kabushiki Gaisha.
Tsuchimochi H. Gary (1993). *Education reform in postwar Japan: the 1946 U.S. education mission*. Tokyo: University of Tokyo Press.
Tsuchiya Kiyoshi (1956, February). Shûshoku o habamareru daigakusei no kunô. *Fujin Kôron*, 60–64.
Tsuchiya Yuka (1994). Amerika no tainichi senryô seisaku ni okeru joshi kôtô ky-

ôiku kaikaku. *Chiiki Bunka Kenkyû,* 123–153.

Tsuda Juku Daigaku (1960). *Tsuda Juku Daigaku 60 nenshi.* Tokyo: Chûôkôron Jigyô Shuppan.

Tsuda Juku Daigaku Sôritsu 90 shûnen Kinen Jigyô Shuppan Iinkai (1990). *Tsuda Juku Daigaku Tsuda Umeko to juku no 90 nen.* Tokyo: Buko Insatsu Kabushiki Gaisha.

Tsuzuki T. & Takamori M (1993). Nagoya chihô ni okeru joshi kôtô kyôiku no rekishi to genjô. *Sugiyama Jogakuen Daigaku Kenkyûronshû,* 24, (1), 295–307.

Uchida R., Yamamoto A., Okuno Y., & Uchida K. (1986). Meiji ki no joshi kyôikukan no kenkyû. *Kanazawa Daigaku Kyôiku Gakubu Kyôka Kyôiku Kenkyû,* 22, 247–264.

Uemura Chikako (1995). Senryôki Nihon ni okeru joshi kôtô kyôiku seido no kaikaku to Amerika no joshi kyôikushatachi. *Amerika Kenkyû,* 29, 95–114.

Uno S. Kathleen (1993). The death of "good wife, wise mother?" In A. Gordon (Ed.)., *Postwar Japan as history,* pp.293–322. Berkeley: University of California Press.

Wasaki Kôtarô (2002). Nichiro sensô go ni okeru ryôsaikenbo kyôiku no tenkai. *Tsuru Yama Ronshû,* 2, 37–53.

Yajima Michifumi (2001). Edo jidai no joshi kyôiku shisô: Buke no kyôikusho o chûshin ni. *Seikatsu Bunka Kenkyû,* 8, 91–106.

Yamamoto Kanae (1974). Meiji joshi kyôiku to kazoku kokka to kateiseikatsu. *Katei Keieigaku Kenkyûkai Kaihô,* 4, 4–5.

Yamamoto Reiko (1995). Tanki daigaku ni okeru kyôin menkyo shutoku no genjyô to kadai. *Wayô Joshi Daigaku Kiyô (Bunkeihen),* 3, 31–42.

Yamamoto Shizuo (2001). Naruse Jinzô to shakaigaku shisô. *Nihon Joshi Daigaku Daigakuin Ningen Syakai Kenkyûka Kiyô,* 7, 1–11.

Yasui Hirotaka (2001). Nihon no josei koyô kanri no genjô to kadai. *Hiroshima Aki Joshi Daigaku Keiei Gakkaishi,* 75–87.

Yasukawa Etsuko (1996, January). Sengo kôtô kyôiku no jendâ kôzô. *Kikan Joshi Kyôiku Mondai,* 23–29.

Yasukawa Junosuke (1980). Meiji kenpô ka no joshi kyôiku. *Hôgaku Seminâ Zôkan / Kyôiku to Hô to Kodomotachi,* 12, 136–143.

Yonekura Michiru (1977). Joshi kyôiku to kirisutokyô: Meiji Taishô hen. *Kirisutokyôshugi Kyôiku No. 5 Kwansei Gakuin Kirisutokyôshugi Kyôiku Kenkyûshitsu,* 85–99.

Yoshino M. & Kusano A. (1999). Sawayanagi Masatarô no joshi kôtô kyôikukan. *Nihon Kaseigaku Gakkai,* 50 (5), 433–442.

Yukawa Tsugiyoshi (1994). Taishôki ni okeru josei e no monko kaihô. *Kyôikugaku Kenkyû,* 61, (2), 129–138.

Yukawa Tsugiyoshi (1997). 1920 nendai no teikoku gikai ni okeru joshi kôtô kyôiku rongi. *Kokushikan Daigaku Bungakubu Jinmon Gakkai Kiyô,* 1–17.

Yukawa Tsugiyoshi (2001). Joshi no daigaku kyôiku ni kansuru kyôiku shingikai tôshin to sonogo no setsuritsu kôsô. *Aoyama Gakuin Daigaku Kyôiku Gakkai Kiyô,* 45, 153–168.

著者略歴

飯田　依子（いいだ・よりこ）

関西学院大学（他）非常勤講師
米国コロンビア大学大学院、ティーチャーズカレッジ博士課程満期退学
（M. Phil.）国際比較教育学
米国ミズーリー州立大学大学院（M.A.）英語教育学
甲南大学（B.A.）英米文学

WOMEN'S HIGHER EDUCATION AND SOCIAL POSITION
BEFORE AND AFTER WORLD WAR II IN JAPAN

2013 年 2 月 14 日初版第一刷発行

著　者	飯田　依子
発行者	田中きく代
発行所	関西学院大学出版会
所在地	〒662-0891
	兵庫県西宮市上ケ原一番町 1-155
電　話	0798-53-7002
表紙イラスト	米田　里菜
印　刷	協和印刷株式会社

Ⓒ2013 Yoriko Iida
Printed in Japan by Kwansei Gakuin University Press
ISBN: 978-4-86283-126-2
乱丁・落丁本はお取り替えいたします。
本書の全部または一部を無断で複写・複製することを禁じます。
http://www.kwansei.ac.jp/press